thai

pure & simple

Warmest Regards

Somk Arpachemele

cook your favorite Thai dishes at home

thai
pure & simple

Somnuk "Sandy" Arpachinda
with Bill Haney

Crofton Creek Press
South Boardman, Michigan

First Edition
10 9 8 7 6 5 4 3 2 1

Published by Crofton Creek Press
2303 Gregg Road SW, South Boardman, MI 49680
croftoncreek@traverse.net

Cover Illustration by Jenifer Thomas
Cover Design by Saxon Design

To the patrons of Bangkok Cuisine and all our restaurants—
they are the pioneers who first discovered Thai
cuisine in Michigan.

CONTENTS

Preface   ix
Introduction   1
Before Your Begin   3
Thai Cooking Tools   5
Thai Talk   7
A Thai Tradition: Loy Kratong   9
Special Ingredients   11
Appealing Appetizers   17
Succulent Soups   29
Savory Salads   35
Magnificent Mains
    Rice Dishes   47
    Noodle Dishes   55
    Stir-Fry Dishes   65
    Thai Specialties   87
    Duck Delights   99
    Seafood Dishes   105
    Vegetarian Dishes   119
Sauces, Curries, Dips, & Dressings   133
Delectable Desserts   149
Bangkok Beverages   155
Bangkok Cuisine Restaurants   159
Specialty Stores   160

 The hot pepper symbol shown at the top upper-right of a recipe indicates a dish that is especially spicy.

PREFACE

Thai is the hottest cuisine in America—in more ways than one.

For the last twenty years, Thai food has grown faster in popularity than any other cuisine. And, if some like it hot, Thai recipes have what it takes to deliver.

It is true that no cuisine has more boisterous personality and flamingly independent character than Thai. Yes, it can be fiery and domineering. And yet it can be sweet and mild. It can be both—and more—in a single meal. One of the most distinctive and memorable aspects of this cuisine is that it has such extremes and varieties—and yet somehow produces a harmonious balance. A truly authentic Thai meal will somehow excite all the taste senses—hot, spicy, pungent, sweet, neutral.

This is a cookbook to help you create the taste of Thailand in your own kitchen and serve it in your dining room. This book has one purpose: to make it easy and enjoyable for you to prepare the same dishes you enjoy at your favorite Thai restaurant.

Many fans of Thai cuisine would like to try some of their favorite dishes at home. But they don't because they have been intimidated by cookbooks that are too complicated, by recipes that take too much time to prepare. Some Thai cookbooks are pretty to look at but of no help to the home chef because they emphasize complex dishes that even Thai chefs rarely use. This book offers instead the classic and traditional fare people have come to enjoy at their favorite Thai restaurant.

The origins in Thailand of this remarkable cuisine extend far back, perhaps more than a thousand years, into China, India, and other distant lands. But the roots of Thai cuisine in Michigan are more easily traced, to the late 1970s and the pioneering efforts of the Arpachinda family.

Somnuk (Sandy) Arpachinda and her husband, Montree, were invloved in the first Thai restaurant in Michigan. In 1983 they founded their own restaurant, Bangkok Cuisine, to introduce diners of metropolitan Detroit to the mysteries, delights, and taste thrills of Thai cooking. That restaurant quickly became the popular choice of diners seeking the authentic tastes of Thailand.

In 1994, Bangkok Cuisine needed larger accommodations for its ever-growing clientele and moved into a more spacious setting on East Maple Road in Sterling Heights. The next several years saw the opening of three new Arpachinda restaurants. Montree is in charge of the Rochester restaurant, while son Pongrat (Danny) manages the Bangkok Cuisine Express in Shelby Township. Another son, Rapeepat (Rexy) is in charge of the area's finest new Thai restaurant, Rexy Bangkok Cuisine, in Royal Oak. (For location and contact information see page 159.)

Now, as the Arpachinda family approaches twenty years as the leading Thai restaurateurs in Michigan, they are recognized for their pioneering efforts in introducing this exciting cuisine to thousands of new fans.

It was only natural for the woman known as the "mother of Thai cooking" in Michigan to want to share her secrets with her loyal patrons and other lovers of the tastes of Thailand. So Sandy Arpachinda has written this book for those who are eager to prepare an authentic Thai meal at home—and to do it easily.

In *Thai Pure & Simple*, Sandy presents the recipes for dishes that have delighted thousands of regular customers of her restaurants in the northern suburbs of Detroit. But she didn't stop there—Sandy has customized her recipes for home preparation. And she sprinkles these pages with a few dishes that are seldom if ever found on a restaurant menu. The result is more than a hundred recipes for the exotic, nutritious, and pleasing tastes of Thailand.

Whether your taste is for fiery or mild and subtle, for a soft rice noodle dish or a sauce that's hot and spicy, this cookbook has offerings for you. And whatever the dish, it can be made from ingredients available at local stores or through direct mail and it can be prepared simply and quickly in your kitchen. (Some local outlets are listed in the back of this book.)

The book also includes descriptions of Thai ingredients, tips on how to use them, and nuggets of advice from a restaurateur who is an outstanding chef in her own right. In keeping with the Thai tradition of gracious hospitality and genial good humor, Sandy offers insights into Thai traditions, legends, and history in addition to her personal comments and anecdotes along the way.

All this is for one purpose only—your enjoyment of the world's most delightful cuisine.

Bill Haney

INTRODUCTION

Many patrons tell me that they would like to cook Thai meals at home but don't know how to start. They have looked at Thai cookbooks and have become either discouraged or confused—or both. Yes, Thai cuisine does have some fancy and special meals that are complicated and difficult to prepare. But most people aren't interested in trying to prepare dishes that would challenge a master chef. No, they have a simple goal—to prepare their favorite dishes well enough to achieve a taste experience similar to their favorite restaurant.

I wrote this book for the same reason my family and I founded our Thai restaurants, beginning with Bangkok Cuisine in 1983. Our goal has always been to introduce diners of metropolitan Detroit to the mysteries, delights, and taste thrills of Thai cooking. This book is another way to do that.

My family and I feel fortunate to have been at the forefront in establishing Thai cuisine in southeastern Michigan. Since we established the first Thai restaurant in the state twenty years ago, more than sixty Thai restaurants have been opened in the area. As new patrons are introduced to Thai cooking, they quickly learn that it is very special. The first thing they notice, of course, is the exciting taste. They are often surprised to learn that there is so much variety and choice. To be sure, if you like it hot and spicy, there is much for you. But new diners soon discover that there is much more to Thai cooking than that. Patrons I have served for nearly twenty years tell me that as they continue to be amazed that there are new taste sensations yet to be discovered.

But there is much more to be said for Thai cooking than the taste. Compared with some other cuisines, Thai food is quite nutritious and healthy and once you have a little practice, it is very quick to prepare. It is also very inexpensive compared with most other cuisines. That is because you don't need expensive cuts of meat or high-priced spices and can produce a great amount of flavor and nutrition with modestly priced ingredients. And there are so many recipes with such a wide range of tastes and textures that you never tire of it.

Thai people pride themselves on their hospitality. It is our desire to make each meal we serve a delight for our patrons. I have the same hope for this book—that it will help you prepare a meal that will bring joy to you and your guests. My wish is that you will savor the dishes you have prepared in your own kitchen, and that you will feel the pleasure and satisfaction that should be at the heart of any dining experience.

Somnuk "Sandy" Arpachinda

BEFORE YOU BEGIN

In some recipes, you can substitute vegetables, but remember that certain vegetables provide a taste or texture that is important, if not irreplaceable. For example, an important element will be missing if you remove the crunch of water chestnuts or bamboo shoots. But celery-like vegetables are often interchangeable; peapods can be substituted for string beans, red sweet pepper for green, and asparagus can sometimes be used in place of other green vegetables.

Utensils

I'm often asked whether you have to use a wok to get good results. The answer is no, if you are careful to use a good substitute and take care to use it properly. A good skillet with deep sides will work well. Any pan or pot in which you prepare noodles or rice has to have a good quality nonstick surface.

Spice

Spice levels are classified as mild, medium, and hot. Yes, you can go in between and have a "mild up" or a "medium up" or even an "extra hot" or "hot plus." Remember that it is usually better if you have any doubts to underspice lightly because you can add chilies at the table. It is a good idea to keep a container of ground chili powder or flakes on the table for those who want to add a little heat to their plate. But if you do overspice while cooking, all is not lost—simply add more white rice and blend it into the portion on the plate. This will reduce the heat in each bite… and of course will also make a larger serving.

Meat choices

Some recipes are better with one kind of meat than another. For example, most people prefer beef or pork with brown sauce recipes and some prefer chicken with the lighter curry dishes. Some dishes are best with shrimp, scallops, or squid. But most recipes can be successful with your choice of meat or even a seafood, or with no meat at all for a vegetarian dish.

Meat preparation

Some recipes call for meat to be prepared a certain way—thin sliced, cubed, shredded. For best results, those instructions should be followed carefully. Remember that beef should be sliced very thin in stir-fry recipes.

One final note

I have included tips and suggestions throughout the book as "Thai Tips." Before you try your first recipe, you may want to skim through the book and take note of these points. There may be something in the last pages of the book that you will recall and want to refer to as you prepare one of the recipes in the early pages.

THAI COOKING TOOLS

In addition to the customary utensils, tools, and devices in any kitchen—such as knives, cutting blocks, pots and pans—there are a very few special items you will need.

Wok or skillet

Fortunately there are now many good choices available for the most important utensil in Thai cooking, the one you do the cooking in. The wok has obvious advantages in that the sloped sides give you more options as you are cooking, permitting you to move ingredients around to different temperatures. But a large skillet can work perfectly fine, as long as you get one that is very large, with at least four-inch deep sides, and the best nonstick surface you can find. The wok or skillet can be used for stir frying, of course, but also for a wide variety of other cooking techniques.

Cooking shovel

Some woks come with a companion cooking shovel. This is essential for mixing, stirring, and tossing motions. In a pinch, a spatula or pancake turner will do the job.

Mortar and pestle

If you are going to crush chilies and mash other ingredients, you will need to have this ages-old utensil.

Nowadays they come in many materials and can be found in kitchen supply stores at modest prices. The heavier the better.

Large saucepan

Get one with a durable nonstick surface and when in doubt, the bigger the better.

Electric rice cooker

Yes, you can do without one, but if you get a good one, you will use it more than you might imagine and it will last almost forever.

THAI TALK

As you visit various Thai restaurants, you may notice different spellings for the same dish. Some spellings are different enough that it is easy to be confused. For example, some menus spell the classic Thai noodle dish as "Pud Thai" while others call it "Pad Thai." The appetizer dish is spelled "Mee Grob" as often as it is "Mee Krob." This is not because Thai menu writers are careless. The reason is that the Thai language has many subtle sounds that are in between letters of Western languages and as people translate these sounds, some will use the letter "G" while others decide on "K," and so forth.

If you listen to the staff (and sometimes the patrons) in a Thai restaurant, you may recognize some Thai words. To most westerners trying to learn a few expressions before visiting Thailand, this musical, ancient language is both complicated and difficult. But there are a few expressions that it may be useful to know and a few tips on pronunciation that may help you to better understand a Thai menu.

The Thai word "sawadee" serves many purposes; it can mean "hello, goodbye, sir, or miss" depending on the context in which it is used. So common is this word in the Thai language, there are several restaurants in the United States named Sawadee.

Thai natives will be delighted that you have made the effort to learn a few words of their language—and they are too polite to do anything except smile if you mangle it.

No or not	*Mai*
Yes	*Krab*
Understand	*Kawchai*
Pardon me	*Khaw toat*
Thank you very much	*Kob koon mark*
You're welcome	*Mai pen rai*
How are you?	*Koon sabai dee rue*
It is delicious	*Aroy*
It is spicy hot	*Ped*
It is pretty	*Suoi*
Not good	*Mai dee*
Eat	*Kin, Rub pla taan*
To be glad	*Dee jai*
Fish	*Pla*
Meat	*Neau*
Rice	*Kaw*
Chicken	*Gai*
Water	*Nam*
Hot	*Ron*
To drink	*Deum*
Good luck	*Chok dee*
I love you	*Pom suk koon*
Don't forget me	*Yaa leum pom*
Good bye	*Laa gorn*

A THAI TRADITION: LOY KRATONG

Thai have a rich tradition of holidays that derive from ancient legends.

On the night of the full moon of the twelfth lunar month (which usually occurs in November), the high tide and bright moon create a romantic setting. This is the day of the Loy Kratong festival, the "Festival of Light." This is one of the two most popular festivals in Thailand and it is celebrated countrywide.

The ancient city of Chiang Mai is among the most popular sites to view the event. Here vessels ranging from tiny boats to large decorated floats are paraded through the streets to the Ping River where they are released to seek their fate on the watery roadway. In the skies above, balloon-like lanterns drift upward into the night sky.

The origin of the festival is lost in the mists of time, which may only add to its allure. One belief is that it is a time of both thanks and apology to Phra Mae Kongka, the goddess of water. In some ways it is a giving of thanks for the priceless gift of water; in others, an expression of sorrow for abuse and pollution of these riches.

The simplest belief is that the festival is observed only to pay respect to one's ancestors.

Others believe the festival springs from origins in

Buddhism. Offering flowers, candles, and joss sticks pays tribute to the footprint of the Lord Buddha on the sandy beach of the Narmaha River in India. It also honors the great Serpent and dwellers of the under-water world, where the Lord Buddha visited. If this is correct, the event owes its origin to a Hindu festival for the god Vishnu, in his realm at the ocean's center.

Still another belief is that the floral kratong is an offering to the pagoda where resides the topknot of the Lord Buddha, cut off at the moment of his self-ordination.

Some historians are convinced the practice began in Sukhothai, the ancient kingdom, in the thirteenth century. The young queen Nang Noppamas was said to have made a small boat and in it placed lit candles and incense and floated it down the river. Her name has been tied to the festival ever since.

Whatever its genesis, Loy Kratong is perhaps the most picturesque event in a country known for its colorful and lavish celebrations. The name actually means "a lotus-shaped object that floats." The kratong, or receptacle, was originally made of the leaves or layers from the trunk of a banana tree. Sometimes a spider lily plant was used. In the kratong are placed offerings such as flowers, food, joss sticks, betel nuts, candles, and coins.

In recent years, modern materials have been used to make even more colorful kratongs. However, this has caused problems as modern materials, especially synthetic foams, pollute the waterways. Recently there has been a return to traditional materials and this lovely festival is again celebrated much in the manner that it was in days lost in the mists of time.

SPECIAL INGREDIENTS

Bamboo shoots

These are the young and tender shoots of edible bamboo plants. It is often best to use canned shoots because you can depend on these for consistent flavor and texture. Fresh shoots, of course, are always desirable and they can be found in stores carrying a large stock of Asian foods. Be sure they are pale yellow and have a crunchy, crisp, mild flavor. Uncooked leftovers can be stored in the refrigerator for about two weeks but should be stored in water changed daily.

Basil

Fresh basil is easily obtained and is necessary for the full flavor it imparts. There are three basic basil varieties: hot basil is good for stir frying; lemon basil goes well with certain fish and chicken dishes; and Thai sweet basil is used as a vegetable, for flavoring, and as an ingredient in curries.

Bean curd (see tofu)

Bean sprouts

Look for firm, glistening white bodies with green or yellow heads and fine hair-like tails. Try to use within a day or two.

For fun, convenience, or economy, you can easily

make your own sprouts from seeds available in Asian stores. Soak half a cup or less of seeds overnight in water, spread on cheesecloth on a flat surface, and set in a dark area (a warm unused oven works well). Or place inside a large bottle and rotate it occasionally. In four to six days they will be two inches long and ready to eat.

Chilies (or chili peppers)

There is a lot of variety in chili peppers, the world's most heavily consumed spice. As with scorpions, the smaller have the most potent sting. Seeds are the hottest part of the pepper. Although hot chili peppers have become nearly synonymous with Thai cuisine, they probably were not known in Thailand until the sixteenth century when they were brought in by Portuguese traders. Many Thai insist that chilies were brought in by Mongoloid people from Central Asia centuries earlier. Whatever their lineage, chilies have become an essential ingredient in Thai cuisine.

Some chilies go by different names in different regions or even when provided by different merchants. The most popular hot chili is the bird's-eye chili (*prik kii noo*), second in heat rating to the habanero. The serrano chili pepper is easier to find.

Take care in handling chili peppers to avoid stinging eyes and imparting their flavor to surfaces where you will be preparing other food.

Cilantro

An ancient savory herb that has become popular to the point of overuse by some cooks. This staple of Thai cuisine has flat green leaves which are plucked off the stem to be used as a garnish or blended into the food, while roots and stems can be crushed into sauces and pastes. This relative of the carrot is available year-round and can be grown on a window sill from seeds, preferably in the spring. For those who don't like the taste, use holy basil, Thai basil, or Italian basil.

Coconut milk

Yes, you can make your own; no, it's not worth the effort. It is far better to buy this essential ingredient, now commonly found canned in most stores. Coconut milk thickens during cooking, giving body to gravies and sauces. Because of the high fat content (nearing 25 percent), the search has been on for a substitute and with good results. Now there is available a lighter coconut milk with half the fat content, produced from a second pressing of the ground pulp that produced pure coconut milk from the first pressing. Another alternative is to use half-and-half which performs very well in many recipes.

Curry pastes

If you like to make it from scratch, curry paste will reward your time. Using a stone mortar and pestle, you can make small batches, pounding and grinding fresh chilies, garlic, onion, spices, and kaffir lime leaves until you have a paste. But don't feel guilty if you decide to buy instead of prepare, because most professional Thai cooks these days also buy prepared curry pastes rather than take the time to make their own. For uses in recipes, see Sauces, Curries, Dips & Dressings section of this book.

Fish sauce

Yes, it actually comes from fish. Small fish are packed in wooden barrels, salted, and the liquid runoff is collected. It is then cooked and bottled and that is the way you can obtain it at Asian markets. It is indispensable in many recipes. Don't be put off by the strong odor when uncooked; that will be subdued during cooking.

Galanga

A root, like ginger, with a thin, onion-like skin, dark

rings, and woody shoots thrusting out from its core. Usually you see galanga as the woody slices in Thai dishes that are there for flavor and not to be eaten. Galanga is another import into Thailand centuries past from Europe, where it was prized as a cure for the common cold, an aphrodisiac, and an aid to digestion.

Kaffir lime leaves

A necessary ingredient in lemongrass soup, many curry pastes, satay sauce, and certain stir-fried dishes. The citrus-floral flavor is unmistakable. Available in imported form from Asian markets only because the tree is so slow growing and so slow to bear fruit that it has not been successfully grown in the continental United States.

Lemongrass

Also known as citronella, this fragrant herb conveys a lemony taste to pastes, soups, and teas. Lemongrass soup to Thai people is like chicken soup to Westerners, as a home cold remedy. Growing in tall, thick stalks, this is another plant you can grow yourself in many parts of America. The lower part of the stalk is crushed, then finely chopped. Easily found in most food stores.

Oyster sauce

This thick brown sauce is made from fermented oyster extracts, salt, and selected spices. It imparts a smoky-yet-sweet taste, nothing at all like oysters. It can be used as a flavoring and also as a condiment.

Tamarind

One type of tamarind is a sweet fruit that can be peeled and eaten. The recipes in this book use sour tamarind. This is the source of the unique taste sometimes described as fruity-acidic that is found in so many Thai dishes. The tamarind tree produces pods that look like big peanuts with a furry brown shell that is hard and smooth. In Thailand, the pods are eaten before they ripen and the seeds are roasted as a flavoring. The pulp in processed in different ways and can be bought canned, dried, preserved, and either green or ripe. Our recipes call for tamarind as a juice.

Tofu

Tofu is now the more commonly used name for bean curd. Once considered by Westerners to be a boring, tasteless, and barely edible product, bean curd has become an essential ingredient with not only the health-conscious but also many others. The growth in popularity may have a lot to do with steps that have been taken to punch up the flavor and texture of the product. Tofu has always been a favored high-protein, low-cholesterol food. But taken by itself, it found adherents only among those truly dedicated to good health. When blended with highly flavored ingredients in a Thai recipe, however, tofu undergoes a transformation. It takes on the flavors of other ingredients while imparting a texture that can vary from hard to soft, firm to spongy.

Tofu is pressed soybean curd, which is ground soybeans and water after the juice has been extracted, and it has been cooked and allowed to stand until it firms up into one of its many forms—sheets, blocks, and sticks being the most common.

For vegetarians, tofu can be used as a substitute for meat or seafood in most recipes. Unused portions can be stored in the refrigerator and are usable until their color changes or an odor develops.

appealing appetizers

Crispy Rolls 19
Tow Hoo Tod • Fried Bean Curd 20
Tod Mun • Minced Chicken Patties 21
Satay • Barbecued Meat on a Stick 22
Nong Tong • Thai-style Buffalo Wings............................23
Koong Houm Pa • Shrimp Wrapped in
Spring Roll Sheet 24
Sandy's Special Thai Taste Pork Toast 25
Mee Grob • Crispy Noodles 26

Crispy Rolls

2 pounds ground chicken
¼ cup rice noodles
¼ cup bean sprouts
¼ cup black mushrooms
1 teaspoon black pepper
1 teaspoon salt
1 teaspoon fresh cilantro
1 teaspoon chopped green onions
2 packages rice paper
A bed of lettuce leaves

5 cups vegetable oil for deep frying
Sweet and Sour Sauce (see Sauces section)

Mix all ingredients except rice paper, oil, lettuce, and sauce.

Dip rice paper in hot water for one second and take out quickly before it begins to disintegrate. Spread rice paper flat for a few minutes before beginning wrapping.

Place about 2 tablespoons of the blended mixture into a portion of the rice paper large enough to shape and wrap into a round fat cigar shape about 3 inches long. Fold in the ends to seal off the mixture.

Either cook the rolls right away or place on wax paper to prevent drying out.

In a wok or skillet, bring 5 cups of vegetable oil to high heat and cook 10-12 rolls at a time for about 5 minutes or until lightly crisp.

Drain on a paper towel and serve immediately while very hot on a bed of lettuce leaves with sauce in small dishes on the side.

Makes 30–40 rolls

Tow Hoo Tod
Fried Bean Curd

2 boxes fried bean curd (firm)
Crushed peanuts

5 cups vegetable oil for deep frying
Sweet and Sour Sauce (see Sauces section)

Cut bean curd in the size you prefer.

Bring oil to a high heat in a wok or skillet and deep-fry until brown.

Serve on a serving dish and top with sweet and sour sauce and crushed peanuts.

Serves 2–4

Thai Tips

Cooking a Thai dinner should be as much enjoyment as eating a Thai dinner. Some dishes are creative and fun to prepare. Others are just time-consuming work. One step you can take to make your time in the kitchen more enjoyable is to prepare larger quantities of items you will be using frequently.

Appealing Appetizers

2 pounds chicken
4-ounce can red curry
¼ cup thin-sliced string beans
½ teaspoon Accord powder
A few Kaffir lime leaves, sliced very fine
½ teaspoon baking powder
½ teaspoon baking soda
2 medium eggs
½ teaspoon salt
¼ cup crushed peanuts
3 medium cucumbers

5 cups vegetable oil for deep frying
1 cup Cucumber Sauce (see Sauces section)

Mince chicken in a food processor until very fine. Add all ingredients except string beans, processing until smooth. Add string beans and mix for a couple seconds only, or mix in by hand so that beans retain some texture. Pour mixture into a bowl and set aside.

In a wok or skillet, bring oil to high heat, then reduce to medium high.

Form chicken mixture into round patties and cook in oil, turning until both sides are evenly browned. Remove and place on paper towels, then serve on a platter, top with chili sauce and crushed peanuts. Place a small sauce dish of cucumber sauce topped with crushed peanuts on the side.

Serves 2–4

Satay
Barbecued Meat on a Stick

Satay is a popular treat on a stick, an unusual yet simple dish that is fun, easy to prepare, and can be enjoyed by almost anyone.

On the streets of Bangkok or Chiang Mai, it is offered by street vendors for a few baht. In Thai restaurants, it is a frequently ordered appetizer. Some restaurants serve it to the table with a small grill so diners can cook it to their own taste. At home, it makes an easy appetizer or cocktail snack, or an offering at a barbecue for each guest to join in the fun and cook his own.

Beef or pork can be substituted for chicken. If beef is used, a cut such as flank steak is preferred; cut across the grain into strips about 4 inches long and ⅛-inch thick. Pork should be slightly smaller.

> **2 pounds chicken tenders**
> **1 tablespoon tumeric**
> **1 tablespoon cumin**
> **19-ounce can coconut milk**
> **4 tablespoons fish sauce**
> **1 tablespoon curry powder**
>
> **Cucumber Sauce (see Sauces section)**
> **Peanut Sauce (see Sauces section)**
> **Wood skewers, 8-10 inches long, preferably bamboo**

Mix all ingredients and marinate chicken in the mixture for at least 15 minutes and preferably overnight.

Impale chicken tenders lengthwise onto skewers, ready to barbecue on a grill for 2 to 3 minutes, or cook in a frying pan over high heat with a little oil.

Serve on a serving plate with peanut sauce and cucumber sauce on the side.

Makes 10-12 skewer servings

Nong Tong
Thai-style Buffalo Wings

This is the Thai equivalent of American buffalo wings. Nong Tong is another dish that is easy to prepare, can be refrigerated for days, or prepared in quantity, bagged, and frozen for easy use later. This popular dish makes a great cocktail snack or appetizer.

2 pounds buffalo wings
½ tablespoon red curry paste
½ teaspoon salt
½ teaspoon black pepper
½ teaspoon garlic powder
¼ cup crispy instant flour
¼ cup water

5 cups vegetable oil for deep frying
Nong Tong Sauce (see Sauces section)

Mix red curry, salt, black pepper, garlic powder, and flour in bowl. Add chicken and marinate overnight.

Bring oil to high heat in wok or skillet and cook chicken until brown and thoroughly cooked.

Serve while crispy hot, alongside sweet and sour sauce for dipping.

Makes 2–4 servings

Thai Tips *If skewers are placed into the marinade along with satay strips, they will become moistened and will not burn when cooking. Otherwise, presoak skewers.*

Koong Houm Pa
Shrimp Wrapped in Spring Roll Shell

2 pounds jumbo shrimp
   (about 21–25 shrimp per pound)
1 package spring roll shells
½ pound ground pork or ground chicken
1 teaspoon fresh cilantro, chopped
1 teaspoon garlic, chopped
½ teaspoon black pepper
½ teaspoon salt
½ cup bean threads
½ cup bean sprouts
½ cup black mushrooms, sliced
Cucumber and tomatoe slices, for garnish
Leaf lettuce, for garnish

5 cups vegetable oil for deep frying
Plum Sauce (see Sauces section)

Mix all ingredients, except shrimp and spring roll shell.

Cut spring roll shells, which are flat, pancake-like circles, into four quarters. Place one shrimp onto the center of the spring roll shell quarter and cover with a spoonful of mixture. Roll toward the pointed end into the shape of a short, stubby cigar.

Deep fry in hot oil until golden brown.

Serve with Plum Sauce on the side.

Garnish with cucumber, tomato, and leaf lettuce.

Makes 40–50 rolls

Appealing Appetizers

Sandy's Special Thai Taste Pork Toast

This simple tasty dish won't be found on the menu in a Thai restaurant. If you happen to be in a Thai restaurant when the cooks and waiters are eating their meals, you may find that this is something they often prepare for themselves. This recipe can be reduced proportionately for smaller gatherings.

1 pound ground pork or ground chicken
½ teaspoon ground pepper
¼ teaspoon salt
6 medium eggs
2 teaspoon fresh cilantro
1 loaf Italian bread, in ½-inch thick slices
3 tablespoons vegetable oil

Cucumber Sauce (see Sauces section)

Beat eggs well in a medium mixing bowl.

In a separate bowl, mix all ingredients, except egg mixture and bread, until uniformly blended.

Spread a thin layer of ground meat evenly onto one side of each bread slice. Dip the side of the bread with the spread meat mixture into the beaten egg mixture.

Bring oil to high heat in a wok or skillet and cook bread and turn until both sides are golden brown.

Place toast on paper towels and set aside for serving quickly while hot, along with Cucumber Sauce.

Cooking Tip: To add a party flavor, you can trim off crust and cut bread slices into shapes, such as circles or triangles.

Makes 20-24 half-slice servings

Mee Grob
Crispy Noodles

This very traditional Thai dish is a little tricky to prepare the first time and have it come out looking like it does in a restaurant. But if you follow the recipe, it will be just as tasty and after a couple of tries it will also look as good as it tastes.

¼ cup tofu, cut into strips
¼ pound pork, sliced thin
¼ pound shrimp
8-ounce can tomato sauce
1 tablespoon salt
4 cups sugar
½ teaspoon black pepper
16-ounce pack rice stick
3 tablespoons tamarind, mixed with ¼ cup water
½ cup bean spouts, for garnish
1 green onion or chives, for garnish
Sprigs of Chinese parsley, for garnish
Sweet red pepper, for garnish

5 cups vegetable oil for deep frying

Combine tamarind and warm water, blend well, strain, and set aside.

Bring oil to high heat in a wok or deep skillet. Fry noodles by adding a little at a time until they puff up, then remove and place on paper towels to drain oil. Set noodles aside.

To make sauce, combine tomato paste, salt, sugar, tamarind, and black pepper and stir until sauce is thick as honey. Add pork and shrimp and cook for five minutes.

Pour sauce over noodles, stirring constantly, until the sauce sticks to the noodles, forming a loaf like a big bird's nest.

Place on a serving plate, garnish with a few sprigs of Chinese parsley, green onion or chives, bean sprouts, and, if desired, sweet red pepper thin-sliced or cut in ornamental shapes.

Garnish with Chinese parsley sprigs and sweet red pepper, thin sliced or in ornamental shapes

Makes 4–6 servings

Thai Tips

Cucumber Sauce makes a small, but nice accompaniment to many Thai dishes. Some diners like to have it especially with hotter or more spicy dishes, including Pad Thai and other moderately or hotly spiced noodle or rice dishes. A small taste of Cucumber Sauce after a mouthful of a hot curry dishes makes a nice counterpoint of sweet and mild after hot and spicy.

succulent soups

Soup is an important part of most Thai meals. In a Thai home soup is not served solely as an early course as it is in Western societies; instead there will be a large kettle of it on the table so portions can be taken throughout the meal.

Tom Yam • Lemongrass with Straw Mushrooms 31
Sandy's Hot & Sour Soup 32
Tom Kha Gai • Chicken Coconut Soup 33
Chicken & Cabbage Soup 34

Tom Yam
Lemongrass with Straw Mushrooms

This is one of the most traditional and popular Thai soups that has also found many friends in America.

1 pound chicken or shrimp
19-ounce can straw mushrooms
1 stalk fresh lemongrass, sliced
¼ cup fish sauce
A few Kaffir lime leaves
A few slices mild ginger galanga
½ cup lemon juice
3 tablespoons chili paste with soya oil
¼ cup green onions, chopped
¼ cup fresh cilantro, chopped
5 cups water

In a large pot, bring water to boil. Add lemongrass, kaffir lime leaves, and galanga and boil for 5 minutes.

Add chicken or shrimp and cook until almost tender.

Add straw mushrooms, lemon juice, fish sauce, and chili paste and bring to boil.

Remove from heat, sprinkle with cilantro and green onions, pour into serving bowl, and ladle into individual bowls.

Makes 2–4 servings

Sandy's Hot & Sour Soup

This is the classic Thai soup that is often a part of a midday or evening meal. This recipe includes little touches that make it even more appealing to Western taste buds.

19-ounce can bamboo shoots
½ cup water chestnuts
½ cup ground chicken
8 cups soup stock
4 tablespoons vinegar
3 tablespoons soy sauce
2 tablespoons chili sauce
2 tablespoons salt
2 tablespoons oyster sauce
3 medium eggs
¼ cup water
6 tablespoons cornstarch

In a large pot, bring water to boil and add all ingredients except eggs and cornstarch. Stir until the mixture is even.

In a small bowl, beat eggs well.

In a separate bowl, combine 6 tablespoons cornstarch and water and blend into a smooth paste, then stir this mixture into the soup and cook until thickened.

Pour beaten eggs over the mixture and stir until eggs cook, then remove quickly and prepare to serve in individual bowls.

Makes 2–4 servings

Tom Kha Gai

Chicken Coconut Soup

2 cups sliced chicken
6 slices galanga
Two 19-ounce cans coconut milk
1 cup straw mushrooms
¼ cup fish sauce
½ teaspoon MSG (optional)
¼ cup lime juice
¼ cup green onions, chopped
¼ cup fresh cilantro
2 cups water

Combine coconut milk and water in a large pot and bring to a boil.

Add galanga and chicken and cook until chicken is tender.

Add straw mushrooms, fish sauce, MSG, and lime juice and bring to a boil.

Remove from heat and top with green onion and cilantro.

Serve in individual bowls or ladle from a large serving bowl.

Makes 2–4 servings

Chicken & Cabbage Soup

4 cups water
1 cup cabbage
¼ cup chopped carrots
¼ cup chopped mushrooms
½ cup ground chicken or ground pork
½ teaspoon MSG (optional, to taste)
¼ cup fish sauce
1 pinch black pepper
2 tablespoons garlic, chopped
2 tablespoons vegetable oil

In a wok or skillet, bring vegetable oil to high heat.

Add garlic, cook until garlic begins to brown, remove and set aside.

Bring water to boil in a 5-quart pot.

Add ground chicken or pork, and cook until almost done.

Add cabbage, carrots, mushrooms and cook until tender. Add fish sauce and MSG (if desired).

Remove to a serving bowl.

Top with cooked garlic and black pepper.

Makes 2–4

Thai Tips

Soup is a very important part of the meal in a Thai home. A kettle of soup sits on the table throughout the meal. Portions may be served at the beginning or ladled out during a pause between heavier courses. Because rice tends to dry out the throat, some people like to eat soup throughout the meal.

savory salads

Salads are an important part of most Thai meals. They bring a nice balance because they are generally at room temperature, have a crunchier texture, add a new array of colors, and of course are often of mostly uncooked ingredients. Some salads can be served as a separate course, as an accompaniment, or as an entire main course.

Thai Salad..37
Apple Salad 38
Nam Sod • Minced Chicken Salad with Peanuts).........39
Larb • Minced Chicken with Coriander Leaf and
Lime Juice...40
Pour Pear Sod • Fresh Roll 41
Sandy's Simple Cucumber Salad 42
Yum Yai Salad • Combination Salad.............................43
Green Papaya Salad 44

Thai Salad

1 head lettuce, cut into 1-inch wedges
2 whole cucumbers, sliced
2 medium tomatoes, sliced into wedges
¼ cup bean spouts
2 slices bean curd, cubed
¼ cup green onions, chopped into 1-inch
pieces

Peanut Sauce (see Sauces section)

Toss lettuce, vegetables, and bean curd loosely and serve on plates or shallow salad bowls.

Drizzle with Peanut Sauce to top.

Makes 2–4 servings

Apple Salad

2 medium to large apples
2 tablespoons coconut, grated
¼ cup cashews, whole or halved
¼ cup chopped chicken
¼ cup cooked shrimp
½ tablespoon sugar
½ teaspoon salt
2 tablespoons red onions, chopped

Bed of lettuce

Toast coconut in a pan with no oil, stirring constantly and remove instantly when golden brown. Set aside until cool.

In a mixing bowl, toss all ingredients except shrimp and place on serving plate on a bed of lettuce.

Top with shrimp.

Makes 2–4 servings

Nam Sod

Minced Chicken Salad with Peanuts

2 pounds minced chicken
¼ cup onions
¼ cup peanuts, split or whole
1 teaspoon ginger
¼ cup coriander leaf
¼ cup fish sauce
¼ cup lime juice
1 teaspoon MSG (optional)
1 teaspoon sugar
¼ cup red onions, chopped fine
1 teaspoon dry ground red pepper
1 head lettuce or cabbage, separated into
    leaves

Fully cook chicken in a little water, then drain and set aside until cool.

In a large mixing bowl, mix all ingredients (including chicken) except peanuts and lettuce or cabbage.

Pour onto a platter, that has been covered with a bed of lettuce or cabbage leaves. Top with peanuts.

Makes 4 servings

Thai Tips

Concentrate at first on your favorites. But don't give up right away if they don't come out exactly the same as restaurant fare.

Larb
Minced Chicken with Coriander Leaf and Lime Juice

This cold dish is a good choice when you will be serving especially hot or spicy main courses or a pungent soup.

2 pounds minced chicken
¼ cup coriander leaves
¼ cup lime juice
¼ cup fish sauce
1 tablespoon ground roasted rice
¼ cup green onions, chopped fine
¼ cup red onions, chopped fine
1 teaspoon ground red pepper
½ teaspoon MSG (optional)
½ teaspoon sugar
A few mint leaves
1 head lettuce or cabbage, separated into leaves

Fully cook chicken in a little water, then drain and set aside until cool.

In a large mixing bowl, mix all ingredients (including chicken) except lettuce or cabbage.

Pour onto a platter that has been covered with a bed of lettuce or cabbage leaves.

Makes 2–4 servings

Thai Tips *Consider the assembly and preparation of the ingredients as an enjoyable creative part of preparing the meal.*

Pour Pear Sod
Fresh Roll

1 box prepared fried tofu (firm)
6 sticks imitation crab
3 cups cooked bean sprouts
6 scrambled eggs, fried
2 medium cucumbers, cut into sticks
6 sticks Chinese sausage (or pork strips in soy
   sauce), ready cooked (fried or baked)
1 pack spring roll shells

Tamarind Sauce (see Sauces Section)

To prepare mixture into a fresh roll, place crab meat, bean sprouts, scrambled eggs, cucumbers, sausage, and tofu onto the flat fresh roll and roll up ingredients to form rolls shaped like long, fat cigars.

Place carefully on a medium salad plate and slice neatly with a sharp knife into large bite-sized portions. Top by drizzling Tamarind Sauce artfully.

Makes 2–4 servings

Sandy's Simple Cucumber Salad

This simple and very easy salad makes a perfect counter-point in texture and taste during a meal. It is especially nice to balance or tone down dishes that some palates may find as a bit too hot or spicy. Its mild and sweet taste also excites the taste buds to higher sensitivity to subtle tastes in other dishes.

2 medium cucumbers
¼ cup red onions, chopped fine

Cucumber Sauce (see Sauces section)

Makes 2–4 servings

Yum Yai Salad

Combination Salad

2 heads lettuce, cut into 1-inch wedges
2 whole cucumbers, sliced
3-4 chicken breasts, cooked and sliced
¼ pound cooked shrimp
¼ pound (about (6 sticks) imitation crab,
    1-inch pieces
1 bundle green onions, 1-inch pieces
8 medium hardboiled eggs, whites only
2 tomatoes, sliced
1 green pepper, sliced

Yum Yai Dressing (see Sauces section)

In a large bowl, toss salad ingredients loosely, top
with Yum Yai Dressing and serve.

Makes 4 servings

Green Papaya Salad

4 cups green papaya, shredded
¼ cup string beans, cut very fine
2 cloves garlic
2-3 red chili peppers
1 red tomato, sliced
½ cup fish sauce
1½ whole lemons, peeled and sliced
4 tablespoons sugar
¼ cup crushed peanuts
Lettuce leaves or cabbage leaves, for garnish

Peel and shred papaya.

With mortar and pestle, mash garlic and red chili peppers.

In the mortar, or in a large bowl, mix garlic and pepper mixture with shredded papaya, lemon, fish sauce, and sugar until fully blended. Add tomato and string beans and mix until uniform.

Serve on a platter. Top with crushed peanuts and garnish with lettuce or cabbage leaves.

Makes 2–4 servings

magnificent mains

Rice Dishes 47
Noodle Dishes 55
Stir-Fry Dishes 65
Thai Specialities 87
Duck Delights 99
Seafood Dishes 105
Vegetarian Dishes 119

rice dishes

Here are five popular fried-rice dishes. All fried-rice dishes are known as "kow pad," with other Thai words to describe the remaining basic ingredients. In a restaurant, if you order just kow pad, you will be served only the very basic fried rice without any of the special ingredients or spices.

Kow Pad • Thai Fried Rice 49

Kow Pad Gra Prow • Fried Rice with Basil Leaves, ...50
String Beans, and Green Peppers ....

Kow Pad Poung Garee • Curry Fried Rice 51

Kow Pad Kra Tiem • Garlic Fried Rice 52

Kow Pad Pineapple • Pineapple Fried Rice 53

Kow Pad

Thai Fried Rice

This is the basic Thai fried rice. Meats, spices, curries, and other ingredients can be easily added to it for special tastes.

> 8 cups cooked rice
> 1 cup chicken, beef, or pork
>   (thin-sliced shrimp, if desired)
> 3 medium eggs
> ¼ cup peas
> ¼ cup carrots, diced
> 1 cup onions, sliced
> ¼ cup fish sauce
> 2 tablespoons sugar
> ¼ cup vegetable oil
> Cucumber and tomato slices, for garnish

Bring oil to medium-high heat in a wok or skillet.

Add meat or shrimp and cook until almost done.

Add onions, peas, and carrots and stir in. Add eggs and stir into vegetables and cook until almost done. Add rice and stir in.

Add fish sauce and sugar and cook until rice begins to brown just a little bit, then remove from heat and pour into a serving platter.

Garnish with slices of cucumber and tomato.

Makes 2–4 servings

Thai Tips

If you have made Chinese recipes, you may have noticed that there are certain dishes that contain almost identical ingredients and yet somehow taste much different. The most important reason for this difference is that Chinese cooks often use oyster sauce, whereas Thai cooks use fish sauce.

Kow Pad Gra Prow

Fried Rice with Basil Leaves, String Beans, and Green Peppers

1 cup sliced chicken, beef, or pork
(shrimp, if desired)
8 cups cooked white rice
A few basil leaves
½ cup string beans, 2-inch pieces
¼ cup green peppers, sliced
2 jalapeno peppers, chopped
¼ cup fish sauce
2 tablespoons sugar
¼ cup vegetable oil
Cucumber and tomato slices, for garnish

In a wok or skillet, bring oil to high heat.

Add meat or shrimp and cook until done.

Add string beans and green pepper, stir in and cook 1 minute.

Add rice, stir, and add sugar and fish sauce, continuing to stir.

Add jalapeno peppers and basil leaves, cook 1 minute, stirring until rice turns brown.

Remove from heat and place in a heated serving platter.

Garnish with slices of cucumber and tomato.

Makes 2–4 servings

Thai Tips *The goal of the Thai cook at home is to plan and time the preparation of all the dishes so the cook can put everything on the table at once and then sit down and not have to get up again.*

Kow Pad Poung Garee

Curry Fried Rice

1 cup sliced chicken, beef, or pork
   (shrimp, if desired)
8 cups cooked white rice
3 medium eggs
1 cup onion, sliced
¼ cup green peas
2 tablespoons curry powder
¼ cup fish sauce
2 tablespoons sugar
¼ cup vegetable oil
Cucumber and tomato slices, for garnish

In a wok or skillet, bring oil to high heat.

Add meat or shrimp and cook until done.

Add onion, green peas, and egg and cook until almost done.

Add rice and stir while adding fish sauce, sugar, curry powder. Cook until rice starts to brown.

Remove from heat and place on a heated serving platter.

Garnish with slices of cucumber and tomato.

Makes 2–4 servings

Kow Pad Kra Tiem

Garlic Fried Rice

1 cup sliced chicken, beef, or pork
  (shrimp, if desired)
8 cups cooked white rice
2 tablespoons garlic, chopped
4 medium eggs
¼ cup fish sauce
2 tablespoons sugar
¼ cup vegetable oil
Cucumber and tomato slices, for garnish

In a wok or skillet, bring oil to high heat.

Add meat or shrimp and cook until done.

Add eggs, whipping in and stirring until done.

Add rice, fish sauce, and sugar, stirring until rice starts to brown.

Remove from heat and place on a heated serving platter.

Garnish with slices of cucumber and tomato.

Makes 2–4 servings

Kow Pad Pineapple

Pineapple Fried Rice

1 cup sliced chicken, beef, or pork
  (shrimp, if desired)
8 cups cooked white rice
½ cup pineapple chunks
3 medium eggs
1 cup onions, sliced
½ tomato, sliced
¼ cup fish sauce
2 tablespoons sugar
¼ cup vegetable oil
Cucumber and tomato slices, for garnish

In a wok or skillet, bring oil to high heat.

Add meat or shrimp and cook until done.

Add onions, pineapple, and tomato, stirring lightly.

Add eggs, whipping in and stirring until done.

Add rice and stir.

Add fish sauce and sugar, stirring until rice starts to brown.

Remove from heat and place on a heated serving platter.

Garnish with slices of cucumber and tomato.

Makes 2–4 servings

noodle dishes

Pad Thai • Thai Noodles 57

Pad Se-ew • Thick Noodles with Brown Sauce 58

Lard Na • Thick Noodles in Gravy 59

Goy See Me • Egg Noodles Topped with Gravy 60

Pad Woonsene • Stir-Fried Rice Noodles.........................61

Drunken Noodle • Stir-Fried Thick Noodles with Basil.....62

Pad Thai Woonsene • Rice Noodles with Egg and Bean
Sprouts 63

Pad Thai
Thai Noodles

½ cup chicken, beef, or pork (shrimp, if desired)
16-ounce package thin rice noodles
2 medium eggs
2 cups bean sprouts
¼ cup green onions
¼ cup crushed peanuts
3 tablespoons vegetable oil
Bean sprouts, for garnish
Lemon or lime slices, for garnish
Fresh cilantro, for garnish

Pad Thai Sauce (see Sauces section)

Soak noodles in hot water for 15 minutes, then drain until dry (about 30 minutes) before cooking.

In a wok or skillet, bring oil to high heat.

Add meat and cook until tender.

Add eggs, whisk into meat, and cook until egg sets up and is cooked.

Add noodles and Pad Thai Sauce and cook until noodles absorb the sauce and become dryer.

Add bean sprouts and green onions and cook briefly until the bean sprouts are cooked. Pour onto a serving platter and sprinkle with crushed peanuts.

Garnish with fresh bean sprouts or cilantro leaves and a few sliced lemons or limes.

Makes 2–4 servings

Pad Se-ew

Thick Noodles with Brown Sauce

½ cup chicken, beef, or pork, thin sliced
16-ounce package thick rice noodles
2 medium eggs
½ cup broccoli (or Chinese broccoli)
2 tablespoon mushroom soy sauce
2 tablespoon sugar
2 tablespoon fish sauce
3 tablespoons vegetable oil
Lemon or lime slices, for garnish

Soak noodles in hot water for 15 minutes, then drain until dry (about 30 minutes) before cooking.

In a wok or skillet, bring oil to high heat.

Add meat and cook until tender.

Add eggs, whisk into meat, and cook until egg sets up and is cooked.

Add vegetables and noodles at the same time and stir in lightly.

Add sugar, mushroom soy sauce, fish sauce, and cook until noodles are soft and tender.

For added taste, allow noodles to burn just slightly, then pour quickly onto a serving platter.

Garnish with lime wedges.

Makes 2–4 servings

Thai Tips *Have a game plan and know what you're going to do before you actually start cooking.*

Lard Na

Thick Noodles in Gravy

1 pound sliced chicken, beef, or pork
(shrimp, if desired)
16-ounce pack thick rice noodles
3 cups Chinese broccoli (or Western-style broccoli)
½ cup oyster sauce
½ cup fish sauce
5 tablespoons sugar
½ cup corn starch mixed with ½ cup warm
water, mixed smooth
5 cups water
6 tablespoons vegetable oil
Lemon or lime slices, for garnish

Soak noodles in hot water for 15 minutes, drain.

In a wok or skillet, bring 3 tablespoons vegetable oil to high heat.

Add noodles and cook until noodles just start to become tender, then brown just a bit to add further flavor.

Remove noodles and set aside.

Separately, in a wok or skillet bring 3 tablespoons oil to high heat.

Add meat and cook until just short of well done.

Add vegetables and 5 cups water, fish sauce, oyster sauce, and sugar and bring to a boil. Add cornstarch and water mixture, stir into sauce mixture and cook until sauce is thickened.

Place noodles on a heated serving platter, pour sauce over noodles, and serve.

Makes 2–4 servings

Goy See Me

Egg Noodles Topped with Gravy

½ pound sliced chicken, beef, or pork
   (shrimp, if desired)
16-ounce bag chow mein noodles
¼ cup mushrooms
¼ cup green onions
19-ounce can bamboo shoots
¼ cup peapods
½ cup oyster sauce
¼ cup fish sauce
1 tablespoon sugar
3 cups water
¼ cup corn starch mixed with ½ cup warm
   water, mixed smooth
3 tablespoons vegetable oil
Lemon or lime slices, for garnish

Cook noodles in hot water until tender, drain, and set aside.

In a wok or skillet, bring 3 tablespoons vegetable oil to high heat, add meat and cook until meat is almost well done.

Add mushrooms, green onions, bamboo shoots, and peapods and stir for a few minutes.

Add 3 cups water, oyster sauce, fish sauce, and sugar and bring to a boil.

Add smooth corn starch and water mixture, stirring constantly into sauce and cook until sauce is thickened.

Place noodles on a heated serving platter, pour sauce over noodles, and serve.

Makes 2–4 servings

Pad Woonsene

Stir-Fried Rice Noodles

½ pound sliced chicken, beef, or pork
   (shrimp, if desired)
12-ounce pack rice noodles
2 cups napa, 1 inch strips
¼ cup carrots, shredded
¼ cup green onions, 1-inch pieces
1 tablespoon mushroom soy sauce
¼ cup oyster sauce
¼ cup fish sauce
1 tablespoon sugar
½ cup water
3 tablespoons vegetable oil
Lemon or lime slices, for garnish

Soak noodles in hot water for 3 minutes, drain, and set aside.

In a wok or skillet, bring 3 tablespoons vegetable oil to high heat, add meat and cook until meat is tender.

Add napa, carrots, and green onions and cook until vegetables are almost done.

Add water, mushroom soy sauce, fish sauce, sugar, and oyster sauce and bring to a boil.

Add noodles and stir until noodles are tender and absorb sauce and become dryer.

Pour onto a heated serving platter and serve.

Makes 2–4 servings

Drunken Noodle

Stir-Fried Thick Noodles with Basil

1 pound sliced chicken, beef, or pork
   (shrimp, if desired)
16-ounce pack rice noodles
A few basil leaves
2 cups green peppers, sliced
⅓ cup fish sauce
3 whole jalapeno peppers, chopped
3 tablespoons sugar
3 cloves garlic, chopped
3 tablespoons vegetable oil
Lemon or lime slices, for garnish

Soak noodles in hot water for 15 minutes, drain until almost dry (about 30 minutes), and set aside.

In a wok or skillet, bring 3 tablespoons vegetable oil to high heat, add meat, and cook until meat is tender.

Add garlic, jalapeno peppers, noodles, and green peppers and stir in lightly.

Add sugar and fish sauce and cook until noodles are soft and tender. For added taste, allow noodles to burn just slightly.

Pour quickly onto a heated serving platter and serve while very hot.

Makes 2–4 servings

Pad Thai Woonsene
Rice Noodles with Egg and Bean Sprouts

1 pound sliced chicken, beef, or pork
  (shrimp, if desired)
18-ounce pack rice noodles
3 medium eggs
2 cups bean sprouts
¼ cup green onions, chopped
¼ cup crushed peanuts
3 tablespoons vegetable oil
Lemon or lime slices, for garnish

Pad Thai Sauce (see Sauces section)

Soak noodles for 3 minutes in hot water, drain, and set aside.

In a wok or skillet, bring 3 tablespoons vegetable oil to high heat, add meat, and cook until tender.

Add eggs, whisk into meat, and cook until eggs set up and are cooked.

Add noodles and Pad Thai Sauce and cook until noodles become dry.

Add bean sprouts and green onions and cook until the bean sprouts are cooked.

Pour onto a heated serving platter and sprinkle with crushed peanuts.

Garnish with fresh bean sprouts and a few lemon slices and serve.

Makes 2–4 servings

stir-fry dishes

Pad Prik • Stir Fry with Green Peppers.............................67

Pad Ped • Stir Fry with Curry and Eggplant 68

Pad Bai Gra Prow • Stir Fry with Basil 69

Pad Prik Khing • Stir Fry with Beans and Curry 70

Pad Namprik Pow • Stir Fry with Broccoli
and Chili Sauce 71

Pad Kee Maw • Stir Fry with Ground Meat and Basil........72

Pad Pak • Stir Fry with Vegetables 73

Pad Kow Pode • Stir Fry with Baby Corn 74

Pad Nor Mai • Stir Fry with Bamboo Shoots....................75

Pad Nam Mun Hoy • Stir Fry with Oyster Sauce.............76

Pad Khing • Stir Fry with Ginger and
Black Mushrooms..77

Preaw Warn • Stir Fry with Sweet and Sour Sauce.........78

Pad Kra Tiem Prik Tai • Stir Fry with Garlic
and Black Pepper 79

Pad Almond • Stir Fry with Almonds 80

Pad Cashews • Stir Fry with Cashews..............................81

Zucchini Curry • Stir Fry with Zucchini 82

Sarm Sahai • Three Company Stir Fry with
Special Sweet and Sour Sauce 83

Sie Sahai • Four Company Stir Fry with
Special Sweet and Sour Sauce 84

Pad Broccoli • Stir Fry with Broccoli 85

Pad Straw Mushrooms & Peapods 86

See also Vegetarian Dishes for all-vegetable stir-fry recipes.

Pad Prik
Stir Fry with Green Peppers

1 pound sliced chicken, beef, or pork
  (shrimp, if desired)
¼ cup green peppers, sliced
¼ cup green onions, cut into 1-inch pieces
¼ cup white onions, sliced
19-ounce can bamboo shoots, sliced
¼ cup mushrooms, sliced
3 cloves garlic, chopped very fine
3 whole jalapeno peppers, chopped very fine
3 tablespoons vegetable oil
A few basil leaves, for garnish

Brown Sauce (see Sauces section)

In a wok or skillet, bring vegetable oil to high heat.

Add garlic and jalapeno peppers and cook until garlic begins to brown.

Add sliced bamboo shoots, green onions, white onions, mushrooms, and green peppers and cook until vegetables are almost done.

Add Brown Sauce and cook until hot, then quickly remove the mixture from heat and serve on a serving plate with white rice.

Makes 2–4 servings

Pad Ped
Stir Fry with Curry and Eggplant

1 pound sliced chicken, beef, or pork
  (shrimp, if desired)
¼ cup eggplant, sliced
¼ cup white onions, sliced
¼ cup green peppers, sliced
¼ cup mushrooms, sliced
3 tablespoons vegetable oil

Red Curry Sauce (see Sauces section)

In a wok or skillet, bring vegetable oil to high heat, add meat and cook until tender.

Add all vegetables and Red Curry Sauce and bring to a boil.

Serve on a platter and accompany with a serving bowl of white rice.

Makes 2–4 servings

Pad Bai Gra Prow

Stir Fry with Basil

2 pounds sliced chicken, beef, or pork
A few bits of basil leaves
1 cup green peppers, sliced
6 chopped jalapeno peppers
4 cloves chopped garlic
3 tablespoon sugar
2 tablespoon soy sauce
4 tablespoon fish sauce
2 tablespoon vegetable oil

In a wok or skillet, bring vegetable oil to high heat, add garlic and jalapeno pepper and stir until garlic browns.

Add meat and cook until almost done.

Add fish sauce, sugar, soy sauce, green peppers, and basil and cook until green pepper is almost done (green pepper should still have just a little firmness).

Serve on a platter and accompany with a serving bowl of white rice.

Makes 2–4 servings

Thai Tips

Careful with those spices! Resist the temptation to experiment until you have mastered a recipe and understand each of its ingredients. Yes, you can substitute if you're out of a vegetable or particularly like the flavor of another, as long as you are mindful of keeping the proper balance of taste and texture and what effect the substitution will have on other ingredients. For example, asparagus is widely available and sometimes a good substitute, but remember that it becomes soft if cooked too long and your timing must be adjusted accordingly.

Pad Prik Khing

Stir Fry with String Beans and Curry

1 pound thin-sliced chicken, beef, or pork
2 ounces prik khing curry
4 cups string beans, cut to 2 inches
4 tablespoon fish sauce
5 tablespoon sugar
2 tablespoon vegetable oil
½ cup water

In a wok or skillet, bring oil to high heat, add meat, and cook until almost done.

Add string beans, water, fish sauce, and sugar, stir in and cook until string beans are cooked.

Serve on a platter and accompany with a serving bowl of white rice.

Makes 2–4 servings

Magnificent Mains: Stir-Fry Dishes

Pad Namprik Pow

Stir Fry with Broccoli and Chili Sauce

1 pound sliced chicken, beef, or pork
   (shrimp, if desired)
2 tablespoons namprik pow sauce (chili paste
   with soya bean oil)
1 cup broccoli, in florets
2 tablespoons fish sauce
2 tablespoons vegetable oil
¼ cup water

In a wok or skillet, bring oil to high heat.

Cook meat or shrimp until almost done.

Add broccoli, water, namprik pow sauce, and fish sauce and stir in. Cook until broccoli is done.

Serve accompanied with white rice.

Makes 2–4 servings

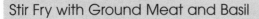

Pad Kee Maw
Stir Fry with Ground Meat and Basil

2 pounds ground chicken, beef, or pork
A few basil leaves
½ cup green peppers, sliced
6 cloves garlic, chopped very fine
6 jalapeno peppers, chopped very fine
2 tablespoons vegetable oil

Brown Sauce (see Sauces section)

In a wok or skillet, bring vegetable oil to high heat, add garlic and jalapeno peppers and cook until garlic turns brown.

Add ground meat and cook until almost done.

Add Brown Sauce and cook at medium temperature.

Stir in green peppers and basil and cook briefly.

Serve with white rice on side.

Makes 2–4 servings

Pad Pak
Stir Fry with Vegetables

1 pound sliced chicken, beef, or pork
   (shrimp, if desired)
¼ cup broccoli, in florets
20-ounce can bamboo strips
¼ cup celery, cubed
¼ cup mushrooms, sliced
¼ cup napa, cut in 1-inch strips
¼ cup peapods
¼ cup water chestnuts, sliced
Few pinches sliced carrots
3 tablespoons vegetable oil

Brown Sauce (see Sauces section)

In a skillet or wok, bring oil to high heat.

Add meat or shrimp to hot oil and cook until almost done.

Add all vegetables and Brown Sauce, stirring or tossing constantly and cook until mixture is done.

Serve with white rice.

Makes 2–4 servings

Thai Tips

The closest comparison between the manner in which people eat in Thailand and America is found in the expression "family style." Often in Thailand food is not served in regular courses, one dish at a time. A dish is served when it is ready. Serving bowls of rice and main courses are placed in the center of the table and portions are taken as desired. Soup is served in a large kettle and is ladled into bowls throughout the meal. Dessert is always last, of course, and is often either a platter of fresh fruits or a simple prepared dish such as coconut ice cream or a custard.

Pad Kow Pode

Stir Fry with Baby Corn

1 pound sliced chicken, beef, or pork
   (shrimp, if desired)
1 cup baby corn
¼ cup napa, cut in 1-inch pieces
¼ cup mushrooms, sliced
¼ cup peapods
3 tablespoons vegetable oil

Brown Sauce (see Sauces section)

In a skillet or wok, bring oil to high heat.

Add meat or shrimp to hot oil and cook until almost done.

Add all vegetables and Brown Sauce, stirring or tossing constantly and cook until mixture is done.

Serve with white rice.

Makes 2–4 servings

Thai Tips

Don't expect that your first effort at home will produce exactly the same results you would get in your favorite Thai restaurant… even if you use the same ingredients and follow the directions precisely. Any kind of cooking—especially Thai—is far more art than science. Subtle differences in the utensils can make a difference. But if you have used the right ingredients in the proper amounts, the difference is probably in how and when you added ingredients, how hot the oil or pan was when you started, and how long you cooked.

Magnificent Mains: Stir-Fry Dishes

Pad Nor Mai

Stir Fry with Bamboo Shoots

1 pound sliced chicken, beef, or pork
   (shrimp, if desired)
20-ounce can bamboo strips
¼ cup mushrooms, sliced
A few pinches sliced carrots
¼ cup green onions, in 1-inch pieces
3 tablespoons vegetable oil

Brown Sauce (see Sauces section)

In a skillet or wok, bring oil to high heat.

Add meat or shrimp to hot oil and cook until almost done.

Add all vegetables and Brown Sauce, stirring or tossing constantly and cook until mixture is done.

Serve with white rice.

Makes 2–4 servings

Pad Nam Mun Hoy
Stir Fry with Oyster Sauce

1 pound chicken, beef, pork, or shrimp
¼ cup mushrooms, sliced
¼ cup green onions, in 1-inch pieces
¼ cup oyster sauce
3 tablespoons vegetable oil

Brown Sauce (see Sauces section)

In a skillet or wok, bring oil to high heat.

Add meat or shrimp to hot oil and cook until almost done.

Add all vegetables and Brown Sauce, stirring or tossing constantly and cook until mixture is done.

Serve with white rice.

Makes 2–4 servings

Pad Khing

Stir Fry with Ginger and Black Mushrooms

**1 pound sliced chicken, beef, or pork
  (shrimp, if desired)**
¼ cup carrots, shredded
¼ cup dried black mushrooms, sliced
2 tablespoons ginger, chopped
¼ cup water chestnuts, sliced
¼ cup green onions, in 1-inch pieces
3 tablespoons vegetable oil

Brown Sauce (see Sauces section)

In a skillet or wok, bring oil to high heat.

Add meat or shrimp to hot oil and cook until done.

Add all vegetables and Brown Sauce, stirring or tossing constantly and cook until mixture is done.

Serve on a platter and accompany with a serving bowl of white rice.

Makes 2–4 servings

Preaw Warn
Stir Fry with Sweet and Sour Sauce

1 pound sliced chicken, beef, pork, or shrimp
¼ cup cucumbers, sliced
¼ cup tomatoes, sliced
¼ green peppers, sliced
¼ cup onions, sliced
¼ cup pineapple chunks
3 tablespoons vegetable oil

Sweet and Sour Sauce (see Sauces section)

In a skillet or wok, bring oil to high heat.

Add meat or shrimp and cook until almost done. Add all vegetables, stirring or tossing constantly.

Add Sweet and Sour Sauce, stir in, and cook until mixture is hot and done.

Serve on a platter and accompany with a serving bowl of white rice.

Makes 2–4 servings

Pad Kra Tiem Prik Tai

Stir Fry with Garlic and Black Pepper

1 pound sliced chicken, beef, or pork
    (shrimp, if desired)
2 tablespoons roasted garlic
¼ teaspoon black pepper
¼ cup green onions, chopped
¼ cup water chestnuts, sliced
3 tablespoons vegetable oil

Brown Sauce (see Sauces section)

In a heavy skillet or wok, bring oil to medium low heat, add chopped garlic and cook until brown. Set garlic aside for later use.

Bring oil to medium high heat, add meat or shrimp and cook until done.

Add all other ingredients except roasted garlic and cook until mixture is done.

Add Brown Sauce, stirring in, and cook until mixture is hot.

Pour mixture onto a serving platter, top with sprinkled roasted garlic, and accompany with a serving bowl of white rice.

Makes 2–4 servings

Thai Tips

One important factor often overlooked in cooking at home is serving food quickly on warm plates. This can make a huge difference—and not just with Thai cuisine. Americans often serve up food on cold dishes or let the dished-up food sit before it is served and eaten. In a good Thai restaurant, the food is placed in front of the diner within two minutes of coming out of the wok.

Pad Almond
Stir Fry with Almonds

1 pound sliced chicken, beef, or pork
2 tablespoons almonds, split
¼ cup celery, chopped
20-ounce can bamboo strips
¼ cup green onions, in 1-inch pieces
¼ cup green peppers, sliced
¼ cup mushrooms, sliced
¼ cup water chestnuts, sliced
Spicy chopped hot pepper, optional, to taste

Brown Sauce (see Sauces section)

In a heavy skillet or wok, bring oil to high heat.

Add meat and cook until well almost done. Add all vegetables, except almonds, and cook until vegetables are almost done. Add Brown Sauce and, if desired, add spicy hot pepper, and cook until done.

Place on a serving platter and sprinkle top with almonds.

Serve on a platter and accompany with a serving bowl of white rice.

Makes 2–4 servings

Pad Cashews
Stir Fry with Cashews

½ pound sliced chicken, beef, or pork
   (shrimp, if desired)
¼ cup cashew nuts, whole
¼ cup white onion, sliced
20-ounce can bamboo strips
¼ cup green onions, chopped
Spicy chopped hot pepper, optional, to taste

Brown Sauce (see Sauces section)

In a heavy skillet or wok, bring oil to high heat.

Add meat and cook until almost done.

Add all vegetables, except cashews, and cook until vegetables are almost done.

Add Brown Sauce and spicy hot pepper, if desired, and cook until done.

Place on a platter, sprinkle top with cashews, and accompany with a serving bowl of white rice.

Makes 2–4 servings

Thai Tips

Trying to re-create the ambiance of Thailand? As with the food itself, the best advice is to keep it pure and simple. There are small touches that will add to the experience of sharing a Thai meal—table decorations, raw vegetables cut into artful shapes on a salad plate, a southeast Asian motif on the tea service.

Zucchini Curry
Stir Fry with Zucchini

½ pound sliced chicken, beef, or pork
   (shrimp, if desired)
2 cups zucchini, sliced
A few basil leaves
3 tablespoons vegetable oil

Green Curry Sauce (see Sauces section)

In a large skillet or wok, bring Green Curry Sauce to a boil.

Add meat or shrimp and cook until almost done.

Add zucchini and bring mixture to a boil.

When mixture is almost done, add basil, stir in, cook briefly.

Serve on a platter and accompany with a serving bowl of white rice.

Makes 2–4 servings

Sarm Sahai

Three Company Stir Fry with Special Sweet and Sour Sauce

This dish is called "Three Company" because it features generous portions of two meats and one seafood. Some diners refer to this as a "love-hate" dish. Many enjoy the blending of meat and shrimp flavors and this becomes a favorite meal, while others try the dish once and don't ask for it again.

½ cup chicken, sliced
½ cup beef, sliced
½ cup shrimp
20-ounce can bamboo strips
¼ cup carrots, shredded
¼ cup peapods
¼ cup baby corn
¼ cup mushrooms, sliced
3 tablespoons vegetable oil

Special Sweet and Sour sauce
    (see Sauces section)

In a skillet or wok, bring vegetable oil to a medium high heat.

Add meat and cook until partly done. Add shrimp and cook until almost done. Add all vegetables and cook until vegetables are almost done.

Add Sweet and Sour Sauce and cook until sauce thickens and mixture is hot.

Serve on a platter and accompany with a serving bowl of white rice.

Makes 2–4 servings

Sie Sahai

Four Company Stir Fry with Special Sweet and Sour Sauce

If you like "Three Company," you will want to try this recipe. But take note that in addition to adding scallops, this recipe also uses different vegetables and a much different sauce.

- ¼ cup chicken, sliced
- ¼ cup beef, sliced
- ¼ cup shrimp
- ¼ cup scallops
- 1 cup broccoli, in florets
- 1 cup baby corn
- 1 cup tomato, sliced
- 3 tablespoons vegetable oil

Special Sweet and Sour sauce (see Sauces section)

In a large bowl, mix all ingredients except meat and sauce, until fully blended. Set aside.

In a skillet or wok, bring vegetable oil to a medium high heat.

Add beef and chicken and cook until partly done. Add shrimp and scallops and cook until nearly done. Add vegetables and sauce, stirring gently, and cook until meat is fully cooked, mixture is blended, and all vegetables are done.

Serve on a platter and accompany with a serving bowl of white rice.

Makes 2–4 servings

Pad Broccoli

Stir Fry with Broccoli

**½ pound thin-sliced beef, pork, or chicken
  (shrimp, if desired)**
2 cups broccoli, in large florets
3 tablespoons vegetable oil

Brown Sauce (see Sauces section)

In a skillet or wok, bring oil to a medium heat.

Add meat or shrimp and cook until done.

Add broccoli, discarding tough part of stems, and cook briefly until broccoli is not quite done.

Add Brown Sauce and cook until sauce is hot.

Serve on a platter and accompany with a serving bowl of white rice.

Makes 2–4 servings

**Thai
Tips**

Oil must be hot, not scorched, before ingredients are added. You can have wonderful ingredients and do everything else right but the dish will be disappointing if you don't add the ingredients when the oil temperature is right or if you cook the ingredients too long.

Pad Straw Mushrooms & Peapods

1 cup sliced chicken, beef, or pork
   (shrimp, if desired)
1 cup sauteed straw mushrooms
1 cup peapods
3 tablespoons vegetable oil
Spicy dry hot pepper, if desired, to taste

Brown Sauce (see Sauces section)

In a wok or skillet, bring vegetable oil to high heat and stir fry meat or shrimp until almost done.

Add mushrooms and peapods, stirring and tossing until vegetables are almost done.

Add Brown Sauce and hot pepper, to taste and cook until vegetables are done.

Serve on a platter and accompany with a serving bowl of white rice.

Makes 2–4 servings

thai specialties

Bangkok Chicken• Breaded Chicken with Sweet and Sour Sauce 89
Asian Barbecue 90
Thai Boxing Chicken• Thai Barbecued Chicken 91
Gang Keaw Warn• Green Curry 92
Panang• Panang Curry...93
Gang Dang• Red Curry 94
Gang Garee• Yellow Curry with Potatoes....................95
Pineapple Curry 96
Neau Yang Namprik Pow• Barbecued Beef
with Chili Sauce 97
Masaman• Curry with Potatoes.....................................98

Bangkok Chicken
Breaded Chicken with Sweet and Sour Sauce

1 pound chicken pieces, breaded
1 cup tapioca flour
1 egg
5 cups vegetable oil for deep frying

Sweet and Sour Sauce (see Sauces section)
Brown Sauce (see Sauces section)

To bread chicken pieces: In a medium-sized bowl, beat egg. Dip chicken in egg to coat and moisten evenly. Roll chicken pieces in tapioca flour.

In a heavy skillet or wok, bring oil to high heat and deep fry chicken pieces until light brown.

In a pot, add equal amounts Sweet and Sour Sauce and Brown Sauce and bring to a boil.

Add fried chicken pieces, stirring constantly, and bring to medium high heat.

Serve on a platter and accompany with a serving bowl of white rice.

Makes 2–4 servings

Asian Barbecue

5 pounds beef short ribs, thin sliced
½ cup teriyaki sauce or mushroom soy sauce
1 teaspoon black pepper
1 teaspoon salt
½ cup sugar
1 teaspoon garlic powder
1 cup Sprite (or similar) soda

To marinade, mix ingredients and place short ribs in mixture and allow to stand preferably overnight but a minimum of 15 minutes.

Barbecue on grill until well cooked.

Serve on a platter and accompany with a serving bowl of white rice.

Cooking note: This recipe is typically prepared with thin-cut short ribs found at Asian markets, but it can also be prepared with standard rib cuts.

Makes 2–4 servings

Thai Tips

The hand is quicker than the eye—this is as true in cooking Thai as it is in performing magic tricks. While you are preparing the ingredients in a wok or skillet, it is crucial that you toss the ingredients properly so they will be cooked evenly throughout. Because you will be cooking stir fry and other dishes at high heat, you cannot let the ingredients stay in one place too long, otherwise they will scorch while other ingredients have not cooked enough. Many people are surprised at how heavy a wok or skillet filled with ingredients is. It takes a good grip and a fair amount of wrist strength to handle the utensil correctly.

Thai Boxing Chicken

Thai Barbecued Chicken

2 pounds whole chicken breasts
1 tablespoon black pepper
1 clove garlic
1 teaspoon sugar
2 stalks fresh cilantro stalk or root
¼ cup coconut milk or half-and-half
4 tablespoons fish sauce
1 bottle sweet chili sauce

Put garlic and cilantro in food blender and process very fine.

To marinate chicken breasts, in a large mixing bowl add fish sauce, coconut milk, black pepper, and sugar, and blend ingredients to an even consistency. Immerse chicken breasts into blended mixture. It is best to allow chicken to sit overnight in marinade, but marinate a minimum of 30 minutes.

Barbecue on grill until chicken is fully cooked.

Serve on a heated platter with chili sauce and accompany with sticky rice or white rice.

Makes 2–4 servings

Thai Tips

At its best, a Thai meal will stimulate your five taste senses: sweet, sour, hot, salty, and neutral. These flavors are unique because they bring together ingredients native to Southeast Asia and blend them in the ancient culinary traditions of Thailand's neighbors, India and China.

Gang Keaw Warn
Green Curry

2 pounds chicken, beef, or pork
¼ cup peas
¼ cup green peppers, sliced

Green Curry Sauce (see Sauces section)

In a large pot, bring curry to a boil.

Add meat and cook until tender.

Add peas and green peppers, stirring gently and cook until sauce begins to boil, then remove from heat and place in a serving bowl.

Serve with white rice, glutinous rice, or rice vermicelli.

Makes 2–4 servings

Panang
Panang Curry

1 pound sliced chicken, beef, or pork
½ cup sliced green peppers
A few pieces kaffir lime leaf

Panang Curry Sauce (see Sauces section)

In a pot, bring panang curry sauce to a boil.

Add meat and cook until tender.

Add green pepper and kaffir lime leaf, stirring lightly until the mixture boils.

Serve on a platter and accompany with a serving bowl of white rice.

Makes 2–4 servings

Gang Dang
Red Curry

2 pounds chicken, beef, or pork, in small pieces
20-ounce can of bamboo strips
1 medium green pepper, sliced
½ cup fresh mushrooms, sliced
19-ounce can coconut milk
A few sprigs of basil

Red Curry Sauce (see Sauces section)

In a pot, bring Red Curry Sauce to a boil.

Add meat and cook until tender.

Add bamboo strips, green pepper, mushrooms, stirring gently. Bring to a boil.

Basil may be sprinkled on to taste.

Place on a serving platter accompanied with white rice, glutinous rice, or rice vermicelli.

Makes 2–4 servings

Gang Garee

Yellow Curry with Potatoes

1 pound sliced chicken, beef, or pork
1 cup cottage-fried potatoes, or cooked
    potatoes cut in small chunks

Yellow Curry Sauce (see Sauces section)

In a pot, bring Yellow Curry Sauce to a boil, add meat and cook until tender.

Add potatoes and cook, turning constantly until potatoes are done.

Serve with white rice.

Makes 2–4 servings

Pineapple Curry

20-ounce can crushed pineapple
½ pound shrimp or mussels
1 tablespoon sugar

Red Curry Sauce (see Sauces section)

Drain pineapple through a strainer and discard juice.

In a pot, bring Red Curry Sauce to high heat.

Add shrimp or mussels and bring mixture to a boil.
Add sugar while stirring in.

Serve in a serving bowl with white rice on the side.

Makes 2–4 servings

Thai Tips

Irish stew is a delightful dish but that is not what you are seeking when you prepare a Thai meal. One of the keys to success in cooking (and not just Thai cooking) is to cook each ingredient just the right amount and have it be neither overcooked nor undercooked. Many vegetables should be slightly crunchy. You don't want to overcook because each ingredient should retain its own flavor and not give it up into the other ingredients. This is also true of the sauce.

Neau Yang Namprik Pow

Barbecued Beef with Chili Sauce

1 pound beef, round steak or similar cut
2 tablespoons namprik pow sauce (chili paste
   with soya oil)
1 tablespoon fish sauce

**Chopped green onions, cucumbers, tomatoes,
and leaf lettuce, for garnish**

On a barbecue grill, cook beef until medium to well done. Slice beef against the grain into thin slices.

In a mixing bowl, blend namprik pow sauce and fish sauce into a smooth consistency, add beef slices, then toss until beef is fully coated with sauce. No further cooking is required.

Place beef on a bed of lettuce and garnish with chopped green onions, sliced cucumbers, and tomatoes. Serve with white rice on the side.

Makes 2–4 servings

Masaman

Curry with Potatoes

½ **pound thin-sliced chicken, beef, or pork**
½ **cup potatoes (use frozen cooked or cottage-**
   fried potatoes)
¼ **cup onions, sliced**
Small handful fresh shelled unsalted peanuts

Masaman Curry Sauce (see Sauces section)

In a pot, heat Masaman Curry Sauce to a boil, add meat and cook until almost done. Add potatoes, peanuts, and onions and cook a few minutes until done.

Serve with white rice accompaniment.

Makes 2–4 servings

duck
delights

Bangkok Crispy Duck 101
Bangkok Flaming Duck 102
Curry Duck 104

Bangkok Crispy Duck

1 duck, whole or halved
5 cups water
1 tablespoon spice powder
1 tablespoon salt
¼ cup soy sauce
Sliced cucumbers and green onions, for garnish

5 cups vegetable oil for deep frying
Crispy Duck Sauce (see Sauces section)

In a large pot, bring water to a boil.

Add duck, spice powder, salt, and soy sauce and cook for 1 hour.

Remove, set aside, and allow to dry, preferably overnight.

In a wok or skillet, bring 5 cups vegetable oil to high heat and cook duck until golden brown.

Remove, set aside and when cool, cut duck meat into small pieces and arrange on a serving platter. Serve with sauce on the side.

Garnish with cucumbers and green onions.

Makes 4 servings

Bangkok Flaming Duck

Don't let the name discourage you from preparing this delightful dish. Despite the name, flaming is for show, not for taste. This is a dish for special occasions and although it takes more time to prepare than many Thai dishes, it does not take a lot of work and is actually quite easy to do.

1 duck, whole or halved
¼ cup baby corn
¼ cup mushrooms, sliced
¼ cup water chestnuts, sliced
¼ cup napa, in 1-inch pieces
¼ cup broccoli, in small florets
¼ cup carrots, shredded
3 tablespoons vegetable oil

5 cups vegetable oil for deep frying
Brown Sauce (see Sauces section)

To prepare duck:

¼ cup soy sauce
5 cups water
1 tablespoon spicy powder
1 tablespoon salt

In a very large pot, boil water, add soy sauce, spice powder, and salt and cook duck for 1 hour. Remove, set aside, and allow to dry.

In a wok or skillet, bring 5 cups vegetable oil to high heat and cook duck until golden brown.

Remove, set aside, and when cool, cut duck meat into small pieces, arrange on a serving platter and set aside.

Separately, in a wok or skillet, bring 3 tablespoons vegetable oil to high heat.

Stir in baby corn, water chestnuts, mushrooms, napa, broccoli, and carrots until vegetables are almost fully cooked, then add Brown Sauce and bring to a boil.

Pour mixture over duck.

Serve accompanied with white rice.

Makes 4 servings

Curry Duck

1 whole duck, barbecued, boned, and cut into
  small pieces
1 large tomato, chopped
20-ounce can pineapple, chunks
¼ cup green peppers, sliced
A few kaffir lime leaves
A few basil leaves

Red Curry Sauce (see Sauces section)

In a large pot, bring Red Curry Sauce to a boil, add
duck and all vegetables and bring to a boil.

Serve in a large bowl, accompanied with white rice,
glutinous rice, or rice vermicelli.

Makes 4 servings

seafood dishes

Seafood is an important food in Thailand. Many traditional Thai recipes can be reproduced very successfully with fish available at moderate prices in imported food stores. Also, most American markets carry catfish and other fish that can be substituted for imported varieties. While the following recipes call for catfish or similar filets, a dramatic appearance can be produced by using a large whole, dressed fish with a texture and flesh similar to the firm but tender filet of the catfish.

Pla Tod • Garlic Fish 107
Pla Jien • Ginger Fish...108
Pla Prew Warn • Sweet and Sour Fish 109
Pla Lad Prik • Chili Fish...110
Pla Choo-Chee • Red Curry Fish
with Green Peppers 111
Pla Dook Pad Ped • Curry Fish with Eggplant 112
Pad Taray • Seafood Curry...113
Bangkok Seafood Combo 114
Pad Pao Tak • Seafood with Light Sweet
and Sour Sauce..115
Pad Bai Gra Prow • Frog Legs with Basil........................116
Pad Kratiem Prik Tai • Frog Legs with Garlic Sauce 117

Pla Tod

Garlic Fish

2 catfish (or similar) 1-inch thick filets
3 cloves garlic, chopped
1 medium egg
¼ teaspoon black pepper
¼ cup green onions, in 1-inch pieces
¼ cup flour
2 teaspoons vegetable oil
Chinese parsley, for garnish

4 cups vegetable oil for deep frying
Brown Sauce (see Sauces section)

Beat egg and dip filets, then coat with flour.

In a wok or skillet, bring 4 cups vegetable oil to high heat and deep fry filets until crispy, then set aside.

Separately, heat 2 teaspoons vegetable oil to high heat and fry garlic until golden brown.

Add Brown Sauce and bring to high heat. Add black pepper and green onions, tossing.

Pour mixture over fish and serve immediately.

Serve on a platter and accompany with a serving bowl of white rice.

Garnish with Chinese parsley sprigs as desired for taste and eye appeal.

Makes 2–4 servings

Pla Jien

Ginger Fish

2 catfish (or similar) 1-inch thick filets
¼ cup shredded pork
¼ cup shrimp
¼ cup mushrooms, sliced
½ teaspoon ginger
¼ cup green onions, in 1-inch pieces
1 medium egg
¼ cup flour
2 tablespoons vegetable oil
Chinese parsley, for garnish

4 cups vegetable oil for deep frying
Brown Sauce (see Sauces section)

Beat egg and dip filets, then coat with flour.

In a wok or skillet, bring 4 cups vegetable oil to high heat and deep fry filets until crispy, then set aside.

Separately, heat 2 teaspoons vegetable oil to high heat and cook pork and shrimp until done.

Add Brown Sauce, bring to a boil and cook for 5 minutes. Add remaining ingredients and cook until done.

Serve on a platter and accompany with a serving bowl of white rice.

Garnish with Chinese parsley sprigs as desired for taste and eye appeal.

Makes 2–4 servings

Pla Prew Warn

Sweet and Sour Fish

2 catfish (or similar) 1-inch thick filets
¼ cup cucumbers, sliced
¼ cup tomatoes, sliced
¼ cup pineapple, chunks
¼ cup white onions, sliced
¼ cup green onions, in 1-inch pieces
¼ cup green peppers, sliced
¼ cup flour
1 medium egg
¼ cup vegetable oil
Chinese parsley, for garnish

4 cups vegetable oil for deep frying
Sweet and Sour Sauce (see Sauces section)

Beat egg and dip fish filets, then coat with flour.

In a wok or skillet, bring 4 cups vegetable oil to high heat and deep fry filets until crispy, then set aside.

Separately, in a wok or skillet, bring ¼ cup vegetable oil to high heat, add all vegetables and Sweet and Sour Sauce and cook until vegetables are done.

Pour mixture over fish and serve immediately.

Serve on a platter and accompany with a serving bowl of white rice.

Garnish with Chinese parsley sprigs as desired for taste and eye appeal.

Makes 2–4 servings

Pla Lad Prik
Chili Fish

4 catfish (or similar) 1-inch thick filets
2 tablespoons jalapeno peppers, chopped fine
2 tablespoon garlic, chopped
2 tablespoons white vinegar
½ cup fish sauce
½ cup sugar
½ cup water
1 medium egg
¼ cup flour
4 tablespoons cornstarch
2 tablespoons vegetable oil
Chinese parsley, red pepper, basil, for garnish

4 cups vegetable oil for deep frying

Beat egg and dip filets, then coat with flour.

In a wok or skillet, bring 4 cups vegetable oil to high heat and deep fry filets until crispy, then set aside.

To prepare sauce, bring 2 tablespoons vegetable oil to high heat in a wok or skillet. Add garlic and jalapeno peppers and stir until golden.

Add water, sugar, vinegar, and fish sauce and cook until sauce boils.

Add cornstarch and water, blend to a smooth paste and stir into sauce mixture and cook until thickened.

Pour mixture over fish and serve immediately.

Serve on a platter and accompany with a serving bowl of white rice.

Garnish with Chinese parsley, red peppers, and basil leaves for taste and eye appeal.

Makes 2–4 servings

Pla Choo-Chee
Red Curry Fish with Green Peppers

2 catfish (or similar) 1-inch thick filets
¼ cup green peppers, sliced
3 pieces lime leaves
Red peppers, for garnish
Basil leaves, for garnish

4 cups vegetable oil for deep frying
Red Curry Sauce (see Sauces section)

In a wok or skillet, bring 4 cups vegetable oil to high heat and deep fry filets until light crispy, then remove quickly and set aside.

Separately in a wok or skillet, add Red Curry Sauce and bring to a boil.

Add filets and lime leaves and cook at low heat until sauce thickens.

Serve on a platter and accompany with a serving bowl of white rice.

Garnish to taste with red peppers and basil leaves for eye appeal.

Makes 2–4 servings

Thai Tips

Texture is crucial. To have a truly successful dish, strive to get the textures just as correct as the tastes. Vegetables meant to be crunchy must be added at just the right time. Meat meant to be a little chewy shouldn't be mushy. Sauce that is supposed to be thick shouldn't be runny.

Pla Dook Pad Ped

Curry Fish with Eggplant

3 catfish (or similar) 1-inch thick filets
2 tablespoons red curry
¼ cup green peppers, sliced
1 whole eggplant, diced to 1 inch or smaller
A few basil leaves
3 kaffir lime leaves
2-ounce Ahisome grachai (also called
    lesser ginger)
3 tablespoons fish sauce
3 tablespoons sugar
½ cup water
2 tablespoons vegetable oil

4 cups vegetable oil for deep frying
Sweet and Sour Sauce (see Sauces section)

In a wok or skillet, bring 4 cups vegetable oil to high heat and deep fry filets until almost crispy, then set aside.

Separately in a wok or skillet, bring 2 tablespoons vegetable oil to high heat.

Add curry and water and blend to a smooth paste.

Add fish sauce, sugar, a few basil leaves, and remaining ingredients and stir to an even mix.

Pour mixture over fish and serve immediately.

Serve on a platter and accompany with a serving bowl of white rice.

Garnish with basil leaves to taste and for eye appeal.

Makes 2–4 servings

Pad Taray
Seafood Curry

½ pound scallops
½ pound shrimp
1 cup bamboo shoots, sliced thin
   to matchstick size
¼ cup green peppers, sliced
¼ cup mushrooms, sliced
3 tablespoons vegetable oil

Red Curry Sauce (see Sauces section)

In a wok or skillet, bring vegetable oil to high heat.

Add meat and cook until tender.

Add all vegetables and Red Curry Sauce and bring to boil.

Serve on a platter and accompany with a serving bowl of white rice.

Makes 2–4 servings

Thai Tips

Many Thai recipes originally called for coconut milk. Those who are especially health conscious may want to substitute half-and-half which may be used without noticeable loss in flavor or texture.

Bangkok Seafood Combo

½ pound scallops
½ pound shrimp
4 sticks imitation crab meat
¼ cup mushrooms, sliced
¼ cup napa, 1-inch pieces
A few rice noodles
¼ cup water chestnuts, sliced
¼ cup baby corn
¼ cup broccoli, in small florets
A few carrots, sliced
¼ cup vegetable oil

Brown Sauce (see Sauces section)

In a wok or skillet, bring 3 tablespoons vegetable oil to high heat.

Add shrimp and scallops and cook until nearly done.

Add all vegetables and crab meat and cook until vegetables are almost done, then add Brown Sauce and bring to a boil.

Serve on a platter and accompany with a serving bowl of white rice.

Makes 2–4 servings

Pad Pao Tak

Seafood with Light Sweet and Sour Sauce

½ cup shrimp
½ cup scallops
4 sticks imitation crab meat
¼ cup peapods
¼ cup water chestnuts, sliced
20-ounce can bamboo shoots, sliced to match
 stick size
¼ cup green peppers, sliced
3 tablespoons vegetable oil

Light Sweet and Sour Sauce (see Sauces section)

In a wok or skillet, bring vegetable oil to a medium high heat.

Add shrimp, scallops, and imitation crab meat and cook until nearly done.

Add all vegetables and cook until vegetables are almost done. Add Light Sweet and Sour Sauce and cook until sauce thickens and mixture is hot.

Serve on a platter and accompany with a serving bowl of white rice.

Makes 2–4 servings

Thai Tips

Balance and counterpoint are important in Thai cooking. For example, if you are offering two main dishes, you probably wouldn't want to use two curries or two noodle dishes. And strive for variety in texture, degree of spiciness, and choice of meats and vegetables.

Pad Bai Gra Prow

Frog Legs with Basil

2 pounds frog legs
A few basil leaves
¼ cup green peppers, sliced
¼ cup flour
6 whole jalapeno peppers, chopped
2 tablespoons garlic, chopped
3 tablespoons vegetable oil

4 cups vegetable oil, for deep frying
Brown Sauce (see Sauces section)

In a wok or skillet, bring 4 cups vegetable oil to high heat.

Roll frog legs in flour, deep fry until light brown, remove, and set aside.

Separately, in a wok or skillet, bring 3 tablespoons vegetable oil to high heat.

Fry jalapeno peppers and garlic until golden brown, remove, and set aside.

Using the same oil, add Brown Sauce and frog legs, stir lightly, and bring to a boil, then put mixture on a serving platter.

Serve with white rice.

Makes 2–4 servings

Pad Kratiem Prik Tai

Frog Legs with Garlic Sauce

2 pounds frog legs
1 clove garlic, chopped
½ teaspoon black pepper
¼ cup flour
3 tablespoons vegetable oil

4 cups vegetable oil, for deep frying
Brown Sauce (see Sauces section)

In a wok or skillet, bring 4 cups vegetable oil to high heat.

Roll frog legs in flour, deep fry until light brown, remove, and set aside.

Separately, in a wok or skillet, bring 3 tablespoons vegetable oil to high heat.

Fry garlic until golden brown, remove, and set aside.

Using the same oil, add Brown Sauce and frog legs, stir, and bring to a boil.

Add black pepper, stir lightly, then put mixture on a serving platter.

Top with garlic.

Serve with white rice.

Makes 2–4 servings

vegetarian dishes

Vegetable Delight 121
Pad Kana • Stir Fry with Chinese Broccoli
and Brown Sauce 122
Pad Ma Kher • Stir Fry with Eggplant 123
Pad Straw Mushrooms & Peapods 124
Vegetable Curry 125
Pra Ram Long Song • Steamed Broccoli
with Peanut Sauce 126
Pad Prik String Beans • Stir Fry with String Beans..........127
Pad Prik Khing Tofu • Stir Fry with Curry, String Beans,
and Tofu..128
Vegetable Curry Tofu 129
Vegetable Tofu..130
Pad Prik Nor Mai • Stir Fry with Bamboo Shoots,
Chili, and Basil 131
Vegetable Red Curry 132

Vegetable Delight

¼ cup broccoli, in small florets
20-ounce can bamboo strips
¼ cup celery, diced
¼ cup mushrooms, sliced
¼ cup napa, in 1-inch pieces
¼ cup peapods
¼ cup water chestnuts, sliced
¼ cup carrots, shredded
¼ cup baby corn
3 tablespoons vegetable oil

Brown Sauce (see Sauces section)

In a wok or skillet, bring vegetable oil to high heat, add vegetables, and cook until almost tender.

Add Brown Sauce and bring to boil.

Serve on a platter and accompany with a serving bowl of white rice.

Makes 2–4 servings

Thai Tips

Simplicity is the key to Thai cooking. Ninety percent of what you do is done with a wok or a large skillet, so that must be a good quality utensil you can trust and feel comfortable with.

Pad Kana

Stir Fry with Chinese Broccoli and Brown Sauce

1 pound Chinese broccoli, in 1-inch pieces
3 tablespoons vegetable oil

Brown Sauce (see Sauces section)

Cut broccoli into very small pieces, taking care to cut stems very fine and discard if tough.

In a wok or skillet, bring vegetable oil to high heat, add Chinese broccoli and stir until almost tender.

Add Brown Sauce and bring to a boil.

Serve on a platter and accompany with a serving bowl of white rice.

Makes 2–4 servings

Pad Ma Kher

Stir Fry with Eggplant

2 whole medium eggplants
A few basil leaves
2 tablespoons garlic, chopped
½ cup sugar
½ cup fish sauce
1 tablespoon mushroom soy sauce
2 tablespoons white vinegar
2 tablespoons vegetable oil

5 cups vegetable oil for deep frying

Peel eggplant, leaving some skin so the eggplant will not absorb too much oil. Dice to ½ to 1 inch cubes.

In a wok or skillet, bring 5 cups vegetable oil to high heat and deep fry eggplant until well done and tender. Drain fully and set aside.

In a wok or skillet, bring 2 tablespoons vegetable oil to medium heat and brown the garlic.

Add fish sauce, vinegar, mushroom soy sauce, and sugar and bring to a boil.

Add eggplant and basil, stirring lightly.

Serve on a platter and accompany with a serving bowl of white rice.

Makes 2–4 servings

Pad Straw Mushrooms & Peapods

19-ounce can straw mushrooms
½ pound peapods
3 tablespoons vegetable oil

Brown Sauce (see Sauces section)

In a wok or skillet, bring vegetable oil to high heat.

Add peapods and straw mushrooms and stir until almost tender.

Add Brown Sauce and bring to a boil until ready to serve.

Serve on a platter and accompany with a serving bowl of white rice.

Makes 2–4 servings

Vegetable Curry

¼ cup broccoli, in small florets
20-ounce can bamboo strips
¼ cup celery, diced
¼ cup mushrooms, sliced
¼ cup napa, 1-inch pieces
¼ cup baby corn
¼ cup peapod
¼ cup water chestnuts
¼ cup carrot, sliced
A few slices eggplant
3 tablespoons vegetable oil

Red Curry Sauce (see Sauces section)

In a wok or skillet, bring vegetable oil to high heat.

Add all vegetables and cook until almost tender.

Add Red Curry Sauce and bring to a boil until ready to serve.

Serve on a platter and accompany with a serving bowl of white rice.

Makes 2–4 servings

Pra Ram Long Song

Steamed Broccoli with Peanut Sauce

Some recipes, such as this one with only broccoli and peanut sauce, are very simple, with only one or two ingredients. It is important that only the freshest and most choice ingredients are used so that the full flavor can be experienced.

2 cups broccoli
2 cups water

Peanut Sauce (see Sauces section)

In a large pot, bring water to a boil and add broccoli, cooking until tender.

In a separate pot, heat Peanut Sauce on low heat until warm.

Drain broccoli , arrange on a serving plate and top with Peanut Sauce with white rice on the side.

Makes 2–4 servings

Thai Tips

The Thai cook is captain of the kitchen. Family and even guests who wander in to the kitchen should be put to work—in good humor, of course. Everyone can have a part in preparing the meal, whether it is setting the table, cutting vegetables, or stirring a sauce—as long as they will follow orders and stay out of the cook's way. Preparing the meal is not work, it is a social occasion, and an important part of family and friends spending a pleasant evening together. Good friends and good food mean a good time.

Pad Prik String Beans

Stir Fry with String Beans

1 cup string beans, in 2-inch pieces
A few basil leaves
6 jalapeno peppers, fresh ground or chopped
6 cloves garlic, ground or chopped
2 tablespoons vegetable oil

Brown Sauce (see Sauces section)

In a skillet or wok, bring oil to high heat, add garlic and jalapeno peppers and cook until garlic turns brown.

Add string beans, basil, and Brown Sauce and stir until vegetables are cooked.

Serve with white rice.

Makes 2–4 servings

Pad Prik Khing Tofu

Stir Fry with Curry, String Beans, and Tofu

> 4 cups string beans, in 2-inch pieces
> 1 box fried firm tofu
> 4-ounce can prik khing curry
> 4 tablespoons fish sauce
> 5 tablespoons sugar
> ½ cup water
> 2 tablespoons vegetable oil

In a wok or skillet, bring vegetable oil to high heat.

Add string beans, water, tofu, fish sauce, and sugar and stir in, cooking until string beans are cooked.

Serve on a platter, accompanied with white rice.

Makes 2–4 servings

Vegetable Curry Tofu

1 pack fried firm tofu, diced
¼ cup broccoli, in small florets
20-ounce can bamboo strips
¼ cup celery, diced
¼ cup mushrooms, sliced
¼ cup napa, 1-inch pieces
¼ cup baby corn
¼ cup peapods
¼ cup water chestnuts
¼ cup carrots, sliced
A few slices eggplant
3 tablespoons vegetable oil

Red Curry Sauce (see Sauces section)

In a wok or skillet, bring vegetable oil to high heat.

Add all vegetables and cook until almost tender.

Add Red Curry Sauce and bring to a boil until ready to serve.

Serve on a platter and accompany with a serving bowl of white rice.

Makes 2–4 servings

Vegetable Tofu

1 pack fried firm tofu, diced
¼ cup broccoli, in small florets
20-ounce can bamboo strips
¼ cup celery, diced
¼ cup mushrooms, sliced
¼ cup napa, 1-inch pieces
¼ cup peapods
¼ cup water chestnuts
¼ cup carrots, sliced
¼ cup baby corn
3 tablespoons vegetable oil

Brown Sauce (see Sauces section)

In a wok or skillet, bring vegetable oil to high heat, add vegetables, and cook until almost tender.

Add Brown Sauce and bring to boil.

Serve on a platter and accompany with a serving bowl of white rice.

Makes 2–4 servings

Pad Prik Nor Mai

Stir Fry with Bamboo Shoots, Chili, and Basil

20-ounce can sliced bamboo strips
¼ cup green onions, sliced in 1-inch pieces
A few basil leaves
3 cloves garlic, chopped very fine
3 whole jalapeno peppers, chopped
very fine
3 tablespoons vegetable oil

Brown Sauce (see Sauces section)

In a wok or skillet, bring oil to high heat, add garlic and jalapeno peppers and cook until garlic begins to brown.

Add bamboo shoots and green onions and cook until all vegetables are done.

Add Brown Sauce and cook until mixture is hot, stirring steadily.

Add basil and pour mixture onto a serving platter and serve with white rice.

Makes 2–4 servings

Vegetable Red Curry

¼ cup broccoli in small florets
20-ounce can bamboo strips
¼ cup celery, chopped
¼ cup mushrooms, sliced
¼ cup napa, in 1-inch pieces
¼ cup baby corn
¼ cup peapods
¼ cup water chestnuts, sliced
¼ cup carrots, diced
¼ cup eggplant, sliced
3 tablespoons vegetable oil

Red Curry Sauce (see Sauces section)

In a skillet or wok, heat oil, add in all vegetables and cook until almost done.

Add Red Curry Sauce, stirring constantly and cook until hot and well mixed.

Serve with white rice accompaniment.

Makes 2–4 servings

sauces, curries, dips, & dressings

Several of these sauces can also be used as dips and dressings.

Pad Thai Sauce 139
Brown Sauce 139
Cucumber Sauce 140
Red Curry Sauce 140
Green Curry Sauce 141
Yellow Curry Sauce 141
Masaman Curry Sauce..142
Panang Curry Sauce...142
Nong Tong Sauce 143
Peanut Sauce...143
Sweet and Sour Sauce..144
Special Sweet and Sauce 144
Light Sweet and Sour Sauce..145
Crispy Duck Sauce..145
Plum Sauce 146
Tamarind Sauce..146
Yum Yai Dressing...147

Preparing Sauces & Curries

Each of the following sauce recipes provides the correct amount for each recipe that calls for the use of the sauce.

To cook these sauces, use a large pot for easy stirring, combine all ingredients, and cook at medium heat, rising to a boil.

Many of the meat and vegetable ingredients used in Thai cooking are the same ingredients used in American, French, Italian, and other cuisines. In part, it is the manner in which these ingredients are combined and assembled in a Thai dish that makes for a different taste experience. But it is something else that distinguishes Thai cuisine from all others. It is the special sauces and curries, the unique dips and dressings that are at the very heart of that unique Thai taste.

Throughout this book, we have made reference to the recipes in this section. While you should use these recipes as described in preparation of those dishes, remember that Thai cooking is by nature a process of exploring and experimenting. You may find that a curry usually intended for a chicken or fish dish goes very well with wild game. Or a sauce created for Pad Thai makes for a delightful dish with other pastas and vegetables.

Very often, diners or even cooks are confused about Thai curries, associating them with curry powder, such as is used commonly in Indian cuisines. Once you have tasted Thai curries and compared them with Indian curries, the differences are unmistakable. The only thing they have in common is the name itself. That is because the word "curry" is an ancient and generic term for a liquid or dry preparation that is made from herbs and spices that are ground, pulverized, or otherwise processed into a blend. Just remember that a Thai curry—whatever the color or the name—is a very special concoction that your taste buds will experience quite differently from any Indian curry you may have sampled.

One thing all curries have in common is that there must be no discernible flavor that stands out from the individual ingredients. By definition, a curry is a blending of flavors to create a new, distinct flavor.

Thai chefs each have their own special touches that make their curry distinct from all others. And even if ten Thai chefs used exactly the same ingredients and amounts, they would produce ten subtly different tastes. That is because the nuances of how and when ingredients are blended and the heat of cooking will make a difference in the flavor or consistency. Many of the curries we use in our restaurants come from centuries-old recipes that have been handed down in our families. I have made slight adjustments in the recipes for these curries and sauces so they will be as close as possible to what you would experience in one of our restaurants, while still making it easy for you to prepare these in your own kitchen.

And remember, any cook must always feel free to experiment—to make very small and careful adjustments to suit their particular taste. That is how new taste delights are discovered, after all. You should do this, however, only after you have sampled the recipe prepared directly as called for.

Once you are familiar with that taste, you might want to experiment conveniently by making up the prescribed recipe, then using portions of it to make two or three slight variations of that basic recipe at one time. Remember, though, that the recipes I have provided here have been taste-tested over centuries and have stood the test of time, so we know that their taste appeals to many people. Therefore, any tinkering that you do should be very, very slight, otherwise you may produce a much bigger change than you intend.

Once you know which variation you prefer, that can become your standard.

Although these curries and sauces are not particularly difficult to prepare, it is often a good idea to prepare a quantity at one time and store an amount. When properly handled, these curries and sauces store well, unless otherwise indicated; that saves time and effort the next time you wish to prepare the dish.

If you were to go to Chiang Mai or Bangkok in Thailand and order these same dishes, you might be surprised at some differences. Sauces in Thailand are usually much thinner than are found in the United States. That is because Thai cooks in America have learned that the American palate seems to prefer a heavier, thicker sauce.

Remember that the title of this book is *Thai Pure & Simple*. For that reason we have modified our recipes for ease of preparation at home. Curry sauces are particularly complicated and time-consuming. The basic curry paste for red curry, for example, requires nine ingredients, some of which are difficult to find fresh, including kaffir lime rind, kah, lemongrass, and coriander root, among others. True, it is satisfying to make your own curry paste from scratch, but many lovers of Thai food have neither the time and patience, nor the fresh supplies to do that.

So, until you become truly dedicated to cooking Thai at home, we recommend using prepackaged curry pastes. These are now widely available in good general food stores as well as all Asian markets, some of which are listed in this book.

Pad Thai Sauce

¼ cup white vinegar
½ cup sugar
¼ cup fish sauce
1 teaspoon salt

Combine ingredients in a mixing bowl and whisk until blended.

Brown Sauce

¼ cup mushroom soy sauce
1 tablespoon oyster sauce
1 tablespoon sugar
1 tablespoon cornstarch
1 tablespoon fish sauce
½ cup water

Combine ingredients in a mixing bowl and whisk until blended.

 Thai Tips *Remember, each of the following sauce recipes is just the right amount for the main course recipes which call for their use as an ingredient.*

Cucumber Sauce

½ cup water
¼ cup white vinegar
3 teaspoons salt
1 cup sugar

Combine ingredients in a mixing bowl and whisk until blended.

Red Curry Sauce

19-ounce can coconut milk or half-and-half
6 tablespoons fish sauce
3 tablespoons sugar
3 tablespoons red curry paste

Blend curry and coconut milk or half-and-half until smooth and of uniform color.

Add fish sauce and sugar and stir until fully blended.

Pour mixture into a separate dish or pot until ready for use.

(If half-and-half is used, this sauce can be stored in the refrigerator for 6 weeks before using or may be frozen if to be used within 6 months.)

Sauces, Curries, Dips & Dressings

Green Curry Sauce

19-ounce can coconut milk or half-and-half
6 tablespoons fish sauce
3 tablespoons sugar
3 tablespoons green curry paste

Blend curry and coconut milk or half-and-half until smooth and of uniform color.

Add fish sauce and sugar and stir until fully blended.

Pour mixture into a separate dish or pot until ready for use.

(If half-and-half is used, this sauce can be stored in the refrigerator for 6 weeks before using or may be frozen if to be used within 6 months.)

Yellow Curry Sauce

19-ounce can coconut milk or half-and-half
6 tablespoons fish sauce
4 tablespoons sugar
3 tablespoons yellow curry paste

Blend curry and coconut milk or half-and-half until smooth and of uniform color.

Add fish sauce and sugar and stir until fully blended.

Pour mixture into a separate dish or pot until ready for use.

(If half-and-half is used, this sauce can be stored in the refrigerator for 6 weeks before using or may be frozen if to be used within 6 months.)

Masaman Curry Sauce

19-ounce can coconut milk or half-and-half
6 tablespoons fish sauce
4 tablespoons sugar
3 tablespoons masaman paste

Blend curry and coconut milk or half-and-half until smooth and of uniform color.

Add fish sauce and sugar and stir until fully blended.

Pour mixture into a separate dish or pot until ready for use.

(If half-and-half is used, this sauce can be stored in the refrigerator for 6 weeks before using or may be frozen if to be used within 6 months.)

Panang Curry Sauce

19-ounce can coconut milk or half-and-half
6 tablespoons fish sauce
4 tablespoons sugar
3 tablespoons panang curry

Blend curry and coconut milk or half-and-half until smooth and of uniform color.

Add fish sauce and sugar and stir until fully blended.

Pour mixture into a separate dish or pot until ready for use in the next step.

(If half-and-half is used, this sauce can be stored in the refrigerator for 6 weeks before using or may be frozen if to be used within 6 months.)

Sauces, Curries, Dips & Dressings

Nong Tong Sauce

    15-ounce can tomato sauce
    ¼ cup vinegar
    1 tablespoon salt
    1 cup sugar
    1 tablespoon corn starch
    1 tablespoon ginger, chopped
    1 tablespoon garlic, chopped

In a pot, combine all ingredients, blend, and cook at medium heat to a boil.

Peanut Sauce

    13.5-ounce can coconut milk or half-and-half
    18-ounce jar creamy peanut butter
    1 cup sugar
    1 tablespoon red curry paste
    ½ teaspoon salt
    ¼ cup water

In a pot, over medium heat, blend curry and coconut milk or half-and-half until smooth.

Add sugar, salt, and water and bring to a boil.

Add peanut butter, stirring until sauce is smooth.

Sweet and Sour Sauce

Crispy Roll Sauce

1½ cups sugar
½ cup water
3 teaspoons salt
¼ cup white vinegar
2 whole fresh Hungarian or sweet peppers
3 cloves garlic
½ cup crushed peanuts

Grind peppers and garlic in blender or mash garlic in a mortar and pestle and then blend with ground pepper.

Add water, vinegar, sugar, and salt and mix until fully blended.

Top off with crushed peanuts.

Special Sweet and Sour Sauce

8-ounce can tomato sauce
¼ cup fish sauce
2 tablespoons white vinegar
½ cup sugar
1 tablespoon mushroom soy sauce

In a bowl combine all ingredients and mix until well blended.

Light Sweet and Sour Sauce

    ¼ cup vinegar
    ½ cup sugar
    ⅓ cup fish sauce
    1 tablespoon cornstarch

In a mixing bowl fully blend vinegar, sugar, fish sauce, and cornstarch and set aside.

Crispy Duck Sauce

    1 tablespoon ginger
    ¼ cup oyster sauce
    ¼ cup ketchup
    1 tablespoon sugar
    ¼ cup water

In a pot, bring all sauce ingredients to a boil slowly over low heat and set aside.

Plum Sauce

6 plums (from jar of pickled plums)
1 tablespoon salt
4 tablespoons vinegar
½ cup water

Seed and crush plums. Add all ingredients, mix, and bring to boil. Simmer for five minutes.

Tamarind Sauce

2 tablespoons tamarind
1 cup water
2 teaspoons salt
2 tablespoons peach or orange preserves
2 tablespoons cornstarch

In a large bowl, mix tamarind in warm water.

Drain off juice through a fine mesh strainer to trap all tamarind seeds.

In a large cooking pot, add all ingredients and cook at medium heat while stirring until sauce boils, then remove from heat and set aside.

Yum Yai Dressing

16 fluid ounces mayonnaise
8 cooked egg yolks
½ cup sugar
1 tablespoon salt
¼ cup white vinegar
¼ cup water
¼ cup roast peanuts

For dressing, process all dressing ingredients in blender at low speed until fully mixed and smooth.

delectable desserts

People sometimes ask why Thai restaurants don't have the extensive menu of desserts found in restaurants serving French, Italian, and Scandavian cuisines. One reason is that there are so many fresh fruits in Thailand nearly any time of the year that if someone wants something sweet at the end of the meal, it is customary and traditional to have a platter of mixed fruit. But that does not mean that Thai people don't enjoy a few prepared desserts as well.

The most popular prepared Thai desserts are quite simple compared with elaborate offerings in other cuisines. That may be because with Thai cooking the other courses have more variety and taste sensations. So the most popular Thai desserts are not fancy and complicated; they need only be a simple, sweet punctuation point to an enjoyable meal.

Here are some of the most common, popular, and easy-to-prepare Thai desserts.

Custard 151
Sticky Rice with Mangoes 152
Coconut Ice Cream 153

Custard

10 medium eggs
2 cups dark brown sugar
13.5-ounce can coconut milk
1 tablespoon flour

Combine all ingredients in blender at low speed for 1 minute.

Pour batter into steamer and steam for ½ hour.

Serve in individual custard bowls or cups.

Serves 6–10, depending on portion size.

Thai Tips

When recipes call for dark brown sugar, it is important not to substitute light brown sugar. The lighter colored sugar does not contain as much molasses and that can make a subtle but real difference.

Sticky Rice with Mangoes

5 ripe mangoes
6 cups steamed sticky rice
19-ounce can coconut milk or half-and-half
2 cups sugar
1 teaspoon salt

Peel, slice, and chill mangoes.

Soak sticky rice in water for 2 hours or preferably overnight.

Steam rice for ½ hour, then set aside.

Combine coconut milk or half-and-half, sugar, and salt.

Add warm sticky rice, stir until coconut milk soaks into sticky rice.

Cover for 15 minutes before serving warm on a platter, with chilled mango slices arranged attractively.

Makes 10–20 servings

Thai Tips

You can't always find mangoes that are fresh and sweet enough, but you can still use this recipe with a substitution that may surprise you. Instead of mangoes, use the custard recipe on the previous page.

Coconut Ice Cream

Ten 13.5-ounce cans coconut milk
Ten cups sugar

Mix sugar and coconut milk and process in ice cream
maker using standard directions.

Makes 10–20 servings

**Thai
Tips**

*Compared with other cuisines, Thai desserts are few and
simple. There are two reasons for this. First, Thai main
courses are so adventurous and flavorful that a small and
simple dessert actually is more fitting than something large
and fancy. Second, in Thailand, people have many tasty
fruits available and elaborate desserts are unnecessary.
Dessert in Thailand will often consist of a platter of fresh
sliced raw fruit, with handsomely arranged yellows, reds,
greens, and other colors.*

bangkok beverages

Beverages with a Thai meal are simple—usually only tea, water, or Thai iced tea or iced coffee. Beer can also be served, with Singha being the traditional Thai beer. Milk, lemonade, and soft drinks are not a part of a Thai meal.

Thai Iced Coffee 157
Thai Iced Tea 158

Thai Iced Coffee

½ cup Thai fresh ground coffee
4 cups water
1 cup sugar
Half-and-half, to taste

Brew coffee.

Add sugar to coffee and pour in tall glasses with ice cubes.

Top with half-and-half, to taste.

Makes 4 medium glasses

Thai Tips
A few years ago, you had to use fully caffeinated coffee in this recipe because decaffeinated was just not flavorful enough. Now the best decaf coffees have enough flavor that they can be used successfully to make Thai iced coffee.

Thai Iced Tea

½ cup Thai tea, ground
4 cups water
1 cup sugar
Half-and-half, to taste

Brew Thai tea.

Add sugar to tea and pour into tall glasses with ice cubes.

Top with half-and-half, to taste.

Makes 4 medium glasses

Bangkok Cuisine
Restaurants

Bangkok Cuisine
2149 Fifteen Mile Road
Sterling Heights, Michigan 48310
810-977-0130
Proprietor: Somnuk "Sandy" Arpachinda

Bangkok Cuisine
727 North Main Street
Rochester, Michigan 48363
248-652-8841
Proprietor: Montree Arpachinda

Bangkok Cuisine Express
43237 Garfield
Clinton Township, Michigan 48308
810-226-8000
Proprietor: Danny Arpachinda and Tong Kue

Rexy Bangkok Cuisine
30923 Woodward Avenue
Royal Oak, Michigan 48073
248-288-0002
Proprietor: Rexy Arpachinda

Specialty Stores in the Detroit Area

Seven Seas Trading Company
21701 Hoover
Warren, Michigan 48089
810-757-1998

Evergreen Supply Company
20736 Lahser Raod
Southfield, Michigan 48034
248-354-8181

China Merchandise Corporation
John R Square Shopping Center
31722 John R.
Madison Heights, Michigan 48071
248-588-0450

Cooking Notes

Cooking Notes

Cooking Notes

Cooking Notes